Songs for all
Seasons

Cover to Cover Bible Discovery

PSALMS

Songs for all
Seasons

PHILIP GREENSLADE

CWR

Copyright © CWR 2003

Published 2003 by CWR, Waverley Abbey House, Waverley Lane, Farnham, Surrey GU9 8EP.

The right of Philip Greenslade to be identified as the author of this work has been asserted in accordance with the Copyright, Designs and Patents Act 1988 Sections 77 and 78.

See back of book for list of National Distributors.

Unless otherwise indicated, all Scripture references are from the Holy Bible: New International Version (NIV), copyright © 1973, 1978, 1984 by the International Bible Society.

Extract from Undeceptions – Essays on Theology and Ethics by C.S. Lewis copyright © C.S. Lewis Pte. Ltd. 1971. Reprinted by permission.

Concept development, editing, design and production by CWR.

Printed in England by 4Edge

ISBN 1-85345-282-3

Contents

Preface

What I like most about the Psalms is that, as Kathleen Norris has said, 'they defeat our tendency to try to be holy without being human first'.[1]

Norris experienced this for herself after spending time as an oblate in a Benedictine Monastery and hearing them read on a daily basis as a spiritual discipline. Philip Yancey comes to much the same conclusion. But, Yancey, one of Evangelicalism's best loved authors, admits that early attempts to engage with the Psalms left him cold. 'People around me,' he recalls, 'seemed to use the book as a spiritual medicine cabinet.' When Yancey tried it, he says, he landed on a psalm that 'merely exacerbated, not cured, my problem'. He then tried an intellectual approach, studying the poetic forms, and various genres of the Psalms. This increased his knowledge but not, he confesses, his enjoyment of the Psalms. Everything changed, however, when he realised he could read the Psalms as you would a spiritual journal, reading them, as it were, over someone else's shoulder, as they speak directly to God. The Psalms, Yancey now reflects, have transformed his spiritual vision and understanding of his relationship with God. Not least, this is because, as he puts it, they 'help me reconcile what I believe about life with what I actually encounter in life'.[2]

First-order language

What helps us, then, together with Kathleen Norris and Philip Yancey, to feel the impact of the Psalms is that, as Eugene Peterson puts it, they are 'primal speech'. If language level three is the language of motivation, and language level two of information, the primal language, level one, is what enables us to express personal intimacy and relationships. Language begins with a wail of protest, a shriek of joy, a howl of hunger pangs. Prayer and praise embrace all levels of language but their underlying eloquence is at this first level of basic speech.[3]

The songs and prayers that make up the Psalm collection are therefore constructed out of the raw materials of everyday existence. But they do not function as a spiritual soap opera. As Kathleen Norris wisely says, 'the Psalms reflect our world but they do not allow us to become voyeurs'.[4] All human life passes before us in the Book but the Psalms will not let us be spectators of other people's hilarity or misery. They rouse us – sometimes exultantly, sometimes abrasively – out of our moral passivity or emotional inertia. They may frighten us with unconcealed outrage or embarrass us with wildly uninhibited joy; but they will not let us go unmoved or stay uninvolved.

Four seasons

So welcome to my discoveries in the Psalms. I invite you to join me in exploring further dimensions of yourself and your God.

I have used the framework of the four seasons as a way of hinting at the different types of Psalms we find in the collection. The four seasons is a metaphor, which reflects a Western European, especially British climate. If it is received as a metaphorical device, I hope that even readers who live under very different climatic conditions – from Norway to Nigeria – will be helped to indwell the Psalms just as well.

In fact, it is just this 'clash of spiritual climates' that makes the Psalms so disconcerting and so bracing. As Martin Marty has fittingly said of the Psalms: 'where they are summery and enthusiastic, they are so with an ease and unselfconsciousness that make modern imitations sound forced. Where they are wintry, bleak, and restrained, they carry one to depths that normal people resist and feel they must resist'.[5]

But it is precisely this dissonance that makes the Psalms such a healthy, God-given challenge to our emotional and spiritual and moral status quo.

God is everything

If we can be thankful that our human personalities are laid bare in the Psalms, much more can we be grateful that God is celebrated so clearly and convincingly. Once when the famous and flamboyant conductor Arturo Toscanini finished a brilliant performance of Beethoven's Fifth Symphony, the audience rose to its feet and applauded rapturously. But Toscanini waved his arms furiously for it all to stop. Turning to the orchestra, he shouted hoarsely, 'You are nothing!' He pointed to himself and shouted, 'I am nothing.' Then he shouted, 'Beethoven is everything, everything, everything!'[6]

So praise must say – and the psalmists do – 'God is everything, everything, everything'!

The joyous paradox is also just this: that in magnifying God we do not become nothing but rise to the full stature of all that we were meant to be.

The chapters on individual psalms began life as sermons or meditations, and I am grateful for all those who first heard them, particularly the keen Bible Discovery Weekenders, who led me to think that God may have spoken through them. I have tidied them up for publication but some of the raw edges of the spoken word remain. I include them as samples of the different types of psalm which I hope you will discover for yourselves, and perhaps, too, to encourage more preaching from the Psalms, a practice which is nowadays rarer than it ought to be.

I am grateful to Mary for being a musically-gifted and praising wife who helps to keep my heart in tune. My friends Trevor Martin, Stuart Reid, and Keith Arscott remain regular means of grace to me. My fellow-workers at CWR are a marvellously supportive group not least because they pray for me and because, in Brenda Sidey's case, kindly forgive missed deadlines.

Thank you for opening this book, especially if you've bought it or been given it. Thank you even more for reading it. May our immersion together in the Psalms and our fresh encounters with the God of the psalmists continue to make us both more holy and, at the same time, more human.

Philip Greenslade
June 2003

Seven things worth knowing about the Psalms

At the heart of the Bible is a songbook

We call this songbook the Psalms. It has been in use by the people of God for nearly three thousand years! Jews and Christians alike have nourished their faith on it and still do.

> The Psalms are 'songs for all seasons' for there is not an emotion of which anyone can be conscious that is not here represented as in a mirror. Or rather, the Holy Spirit has here drawn to the life all the griefs, sorrows, fears, doubts, hopes, cares, perplexities, in short, all the distracting emotions with which the minds of men are wont to be agitated.
>
> (John Calvin)

> The psalter is the book of all saints; and everyone, in whatever situation he may be, finds in that situation Psalms and words that fit his case, that suit him as if they were put there just for his sake, so that he could not put it better himself, or find or wish for anything better.
>
> (Martin Luther)

The Psalms are covenantal

The Psalms do fit almost all seasons of the soul. But we misunderstand them if we read them as merely the typical expressions of religious-minded people everywhere. To the contrary, the Psalms, while expressing universal concerns, are the obligated worship of a particular people, Israel, in a definite covenant relationship with the LORD who is Yahweh. The NIV translators indicate for us when the text mentions God's covenant name, Yahweh, as revealed to Moses at the burning bush (Exod. 3) by using upper case letters, LORD. When the Hebrew word Adonai occurs this is usually translated as Lord in upper and lower case.

There were several types of covenant agreement in use in the diplomacy of the ancient world. The one that most closely approximates to the form in which God's commitment to Israel is framed is what is known as a 'suzerainty-vassal' type treaty. This was the kind of covenant drawn up by a conquering lord in which he pledges himself to protect his subjugated people and puts them under lawful obligation to honour and praise him. Yahweh, who has paradoxically freed the Israelites from slavery, binds Himself in solemn covenant to be their God and own them as His people.[7]

The Psalms are liturgical – the hymnbook of the Old Testament liturgy and public worship

The Jerusalem Temple was a busy place with twice-daily, weekly, monthly, and annual services and festivals.

- Longing for Jerusalem and the Temple-evoked worship: see Psalms 42; 84.
- The bringing up of the ark of the covenant – the sacred box at which God was deemed to be especially present – was a

particularly significant event recalled in subsequent ritual; see Psalms 95:1ff; 100; 132:6–9.

- The laws of entrance to the sanctuary are spelled out in various Psalms: eg 15; 24:1–6.
- Snatches of the original entrance liturgy may well be preserved in Psalm 24:7–10.
- The movement of processional worship is echoed in the dramatic song of Psalm 68.
- Prophetic or priestly interjection in the midst of worship may be captured for us in Psalms 12:5; 32:8; 50:7; 60:6; 81:6; 91:14.
- The demanding but eagerly awaited pilgrimage to Jerusalem for each of the annual festivals is vividly reflected in the songs of ascent in Psalms 120–134.

As Eugene Peterson wisely comments,

Left to ourselves we are never more selfish than when we pray. With God as the Great Sympathiser, the Great Giver, the great Promiser we go to our knees and indulge every impulse for gratification. But the Psalms that teach us to pray never leave us to ourselves; they embed all our prayers in liturgy. Liturgy defends us against the commonest diseases of prayer: the tyranny of our emotions, the isolationism of our pride. Liturgy pulls us out of the tiresome business of looking after ourselves and into the exhilarating enterprise of seeing and participating in what God is doing.[8]

The Psalms are a literary construction

(a) The Psalm collection is made up of five 'books' which perhaps are meant to match the first five books of the Bible, known as the Pentateuch. These Psalm books are: 2–41; 42–72; 73–89; 90–106; 107–150. The close of each 'book' is marked by a doxology.

(b) Gerald Wilson has nuanced this to suggest that the kingship theme is emphasised.

He notes that a royal psalm ends each book up to Book Three where Psalm 89 rehearses the privileges of the Davidic Covenant of kingship but then mourns the failure of kingship in Israel. Book Four then is presented as the answer to the dilemma by confidently asserting that 'the Lord reigns'. The collection may well properly end, suggests Wilson, with Psalm 144 (v.15 'blessed ...'; see Psa. 1:1; 2:12) and Psalm 145 which extols the kingdom of God.

(c) Within these are smaller collections. For example there are a number of psalms ascribed to Asaph (50; 73–80), others to Korah (42–49; 84–85; 87–88), and a grouping together of what are usually called 'songs of ascent' (120–134).

(d) Psalm 1 sets up the necessary spiritual and moral choices which must be made by anyone intending to enter the sanctuary (of the Psalms themselves or the Temple) to worship. Together with Psalm 2 it forms an important doorway of understanding through which to explore the whole collection. We shall say more on this in the next chapter.

(e) The Psalm titles are later additions to the text and are an early and interesting but not infallible guide to the setting of the Psalms. The historical background to some psalms is clear (eg Psa. 51) but in most cases has been obscured by long usage in worship. Although there is no scholarly consensus on the meaning of the musical and technical terms scattered throughout the collection, what is clear is that the term 'psalms' is a trans-literation of a Greek word *psalmoi* which originally meant the 'striking of fingers on a string' in connection with singing. So 'Psalms' means 'sacred songs sung to musical accompaniment'.[9]

The Psalms are poetry and 'Poems appeal to the whole person in a way that prose does not'[10]

For an example outside the Psalms, consider the impact made on you by the prose report of the Exodus in Exodus 14:26–31 and its celebration in poetic song by Moses and Miriam in Exodus 15!

Characteristic is the use of imagery so that we feel what is being said. Here, as Kathleen Norris puts it, we find 'words that resonate with the senses as they aim for the stars'.[11] God's providential care is likened to a shepherd leading his flock beside still waters and through shadowed valleys. To pursue God with spiritual desire is to be like a deer longing for flowing streams. God is rock and river, fountain and fortress, the fixed point of safety and the flowing source of vitality. Such picturesque language serves a double function: it 'forms our feeling in the process of expressing it'.[12]

Another well-noted feature of Hebrew poetry is the use of parallelism. This is a two-line pattern of writing in which the second line matches the first in some way. The parallelism can be

- **synonymous,** where the second line says the same as the first in different words:
  eg Psalm 2:1 *'Why do the nations conspire and the peoples plot in vain?'*

- **contrasting:**
  eg Psalm 1:6 *'For the LORD watches over the righteous, but the way of the wicked will perish.'*

- **climactic** where the second line adds to the first:
  eg Psalm 96:7 *'Ascribe to the LORD, O families of nations, ascribe to the LORD, glory and strength.'*

- **expansive** where the second line enlarges on the first:

eg Psalm 95:3 *'For the* LORD *is a great God, the great King above all gods.'*

- **explanatory** where the second line explains the imagery of the first:
eg Psalm 42:1 *'As the deer pants for streams of water, so my soul longs for you, O God.'*

By such intriguing and varied use of these poetic styles, we are enabled, as Ronald Allen suggests, to hear 'in stereo'.[13]

The Psalms are Davidic in the broadest sense

This is not in the sense that David wrote them all but because he set the tone and style for Israel's worship and was the fountain-head of Israel's praise.

- He had unusual musical gifts: 1 Samuel 16:18, 23; 2 Samuel 23:1.
- He instituted praise in Israel: 1 Chronicles 15–16.
- He was the benchmark for later reforms or the recovery of worship in Israel: 2 Chronicles 29:27; Nehemiah 12:36.

The Davidic roots of praise in Israel are re-emphasised after the Exile by the Chronicler (1 Chron. 15–16; see 2 Sam. 6). According to his retrospective account, David made a remarkable innovation in Israel's worship. He left the Mosaic tabernacle at Gibeon (1 Chron. 16:39) and instead instituted non-sacrificial praise in Jerusalem. This departure from the animal sacrifices and offerings laid down in the Torah put the emphasis on the 'sacrifice of praise'.

David's action gave rise to psalmody (1 Chron. 16:7–36). His bold move opened up a unique 33-year period in Israel's history that became the standard by which later worship was measured, and that proved to be prophetic of the true spiritual worship of the kingdom of God.

Old Testament scholar Craig Broyles suggests another way in which the Psalms are 'Davidic', which has to do with the psalm superscriptions attributing Psalms to, or connecting them, with David. The terminology found in the superscriptions is paralleled in 1 and 2 Chronicles. Not until the Exile or immediately post-Exilic period were the first five books of the Bible called the 'Book of Moses', which stamped them with his authority. Similarly with David. When the Temple was destroyed, the Psalms were rescued and taken into Exile as literature. Set alongside the other sacred writings they became part of canonical scripture. Keen to instruct the post-Exilic generation in ways of worship, the Chronicler, for example, retells the story of David told in 1 and 2 Samuel. 'The historical superscriptions thus invite readers to engage in a new way of reading the Psalms, that is, to read "the Psalms of David" as the Psalms authored "by" David. We may thus read Psalms as liturgical texts for public worship and as model prayers of David for private use.'[14]

Whatever the truth of this, one thing is clear: the first priority of Davidic worship was the royal presence of God in the praising congregation – symbolised by the ark of the covenant. Its chief characteristics were exuberant and corporate singing and praise.

The psalmody that had its original roots in David's time, talent and devotion developed over the centuries

It developed as individual Israelites and Israel's national representatives reached out to respond to God in various circumstances; all of which is reflected in the variety of Psalm types for different situations:

Hymns of praise

These celebrate who God is and what He characteristically does.

In particular Israel rejoices in creation as the handiwork of the One Creator God, and heralds His creative wisdom to the world. Above all, through these songs of undiluted praise Israel shows her delight at being in covenant relationship with God, and being the privileged people He loves and sustains.

Laments, both individual and corporate

These prayers and songs reflect the dark side of experience.

In them the psalmists confess sin and guilt and seek forgiveness. In these songs we find the doubt, and questioning and fear that is squeezed out of us under pressure of pain, or threat of death. Through these songs the psalmist can even release – and release on to God – anger, bitterness, resentment, and sometimes desire for revenge.

Thanksgiving psalms

These are songs of trust and confidence sung by those who are profoundly grateful for God's acts of grace and mercy. The harvest is safely gathered in, the battle is won, the rescue mission is successful, let the redeemed of the Lord say: 'Give thanks to the LORD, for he is good; his love endures for ever.' Psalm 107 is a wonderful example of a roll-call of testimonies to God's saving grace. Wanderers are brought home from exile, prisoners are set free, the sick brought low with self-inflicted and nearly fatal diseases are healed, the drowning at their wit's end are dramatically delivered. These songs traverse the emotional spectrum from mourningto joy as they tell the stories of salvation. Desperate people prayed desperate prayers. The Lord heard and answered and saved them from their troubles. Their sense of relief is almost palpable.

Royal psalms of enthronement and future hope and aspiration

In Psalms 2-72 the Davidic kingship is celebrated as God's representative rule in Zion. But, as we have already noted, the loss of the monarchy at the time of the Exile leads to a re-evaluation of the place and style of kingship (Psa. 89). All eyes now look to God alone as King and hope rests with Him as to how He can redeem the office of kingship for the future plan of salvation.

We may note two further points here. Firstly, the refocusing of the trust in kingship intensifies hope as the collection draws to a close. For this reason I have grouped with the royal psalms those other songs that express deep longing for God (Psa. 42; 63 and so on) and those songs that accompany the pilgrims who are eager to encounter the royal presence of God at the festival in Zion (Psa. 120-134).[15] Secondly, although laments outnumber praise as a whole, praise intensifies as the collection comes to an end. The last five psalms form a climax of praise so that each of them begins and ends with a stirring 'hallelujah' – 'Praise the Lord'! Prayer is finally consummated in praise.

'Praise is the duty and delight, the ultimate vocation of the human community; indeed of all creation. Yes, all of life is aimed toward God and finally exists for the sake of God.'[16]

The praise of God is not a passing fancy! It is one of the most elemental, fundamental, and necessary factors of the life of faith in this and any age. It is the goal and direction of all creation. The praise of God is the occupation of his holy angels. The praise of God is the purpose of man. The praise of God is the end result of all God's wonders, all his being, and all his acts. If man will not praise God, the very stones will! He has redeemed us for the praise of his glory (Eph.1:6–15). This is no fad![17]

Why the Psalms?
Eugene Peterson gives us an answer:

If we wish to develop in the life of faith, to mature in our humanity, and to glorify God with our entire heart, mind, soul, and strength, the Psalms are necessary ... In a world of prayers that indulge the religious ego and cultivate passionate longings, the Psalms stand out with a sort of angular austerity. The Psalms are acts of obedience, answering the God who has addressed us. God's word precedes these words: these prayers don't seek God, they respond to the God who seeks us.[18]

It is vital, therefore, that we see the Psalms, set within the inspired text of Scripture, as part of God's self-revelation. They reveal the worthiness of the God we worship, and how and when we may respond to Him in worship through praise and prayer.

Double Doorway to the Psalms (Psalms 1 and 2)

Psalm 1

[1]Blessed is the man
  who does not walk in the
    counsel of the wicked
or stand in the way of sinners
  or sit in the seat of mockers.
[2]But his delight is in the law of the
    LORD,
  and on his law he meditates
    day and night.
[3]He is like a tree planted by
    streams of water,
  which yields its fruit in season
and whose leaf does not wither.
  Whatever he does prospers.

[4]Not so the wicked!
  They are like chaff
    that the wind blows away.
[5]Therefore the wicked will not
    stand in the judgment,
  nor sinners in the assembly of
    the righteous.

Psalm 2

[1]Why do the nations conspire
  and the peoples plot in vain?
[2]The kings of the earth take their
    stand
  and the rulers gather together
    against the LORD
  and against his Anointed One.
[3]'Let us break their chains,' they
    say,
  'and throw off their fetters.'

[4]The One enthroned in heaven
    laughs;
  the LORD scoffs at them.
[5]Then he rebukes them in his
    anger
  and terrifies them in his wrath,
    saying,
[6]'I have installed my King
  on Zion, my holy hill.'

⁶For the LORD watches over the
    way of the righteous,
but the way of the wicked
    will perish.

⁷I will proclaim the decree of the
    LORD:

He said to me, 'You are my Son;
    today I have become your
    Father.
⁸Ask of me,
    and I will make the nations
    your inheritance,
    the ends of the earth your
    possession.
⁹You will rule them with an iron
    sceptre;
    you will dash them to pieces
    like pottery.'

¹⁰Therefore, you kings, be wise;
    be warned, you rulers of the
    earth.
¹¹Serve the LORD with fear
    and rejoice with trembling.
¹²Kiss the Son, lest he be angry
    and you be destroyed in your
    way,
    for his wrath can flare up in a
    moment.
    Blessed are all who take refuge
    in him.

THE FIRST TWO PSALMS FORM A 'DOUBLE DOORWAY' introducing us to the whole Psalm collection.

These two psalms are obvious twins, bracketed by similar beatitudes:

- 'Blessed is the man who does not walk in the counsel of the wicked ...' (1:1)
- 'Blessed are all who take refuge in him.' (2:12)

Taken together these two psalms alert us to two main requisites of genuinely biblical worship.

Firstly, in order to pray and to praise we need to know that God exists and is the rewarder of those who seek Him in this way. Jesus was only summing up the Jewish and biblical tradition when He said, we worship a God we know (John 4:22). Old Testament worshippers were confident in approaching God precisely because they believed they were not coming to an unknown God. Their confidence was based on the uniquely biblical conviction that God had taken the initiative and made Himself known to them. He had done this chiefly in and through His Word. It is with His self-revealing Word that Psalm 1 begins. God has given Israel the Torah.

Torah has a broader meaning than law or set of laws. No one 'delights in' or 'meditates day and night' on legal intricacies except lawyers. Rather the Torah is equivalent to the first five books of the Bible and contains the founding stories of salvation, as well as commandments, that defined Israel's life with God. Torah therefore denotes teaching or – to use Clinton McCann's phrase – 'covenant-instruction'. I agree with him when he suggests that translating 'Torah' as 'covenant-instruction' gives a whole new flavour to the psalm.[19]

Once God has spoken covenantally, everything else is response. The choice is to hear and respond to God's self-revelation. The righteous man is the one who hears God's Word, bends his whole life in a Godward direction, and ventures boldly and obediently on the covenant partnership with God.

God had made a deep covenant commitment to His people. Israel's first duty was to love God in return. God was their King and covenant Lord. The first thing due to Him was heartfelt praise and adoration. The covenant bond was so firm that biblical believers could afford to eschew flattery. The covenant relationship encouraged them to express themselves openly to God. It emboldened them to question God, and even get angry with God. Covenant love gave them the freedom to talk to God with raw-edged realism. They complained without embarrassment, just as they rejoiced without inhibition.

Psalm 1 emphasises, then, that to choose to walk in the way of Torah is to choose to walk and worship, pray and praise, in response to God's own self-revelation.

Psalms as Torah

But there is a further, fascinating, point that is being made by the inclusion of Psalm 1 at the head of the collection. Not only is Israel's worship as reflected in the Psalms a response to God's self-revelation, it is now to be viewed as forming part of that revelation! Psalm 1 is intended to identify the function of the whole Psalm collection as not merely a record of personal or corporate experiences of God, or even of testimonies to God in song and poetry but as the 'Torah of the Lord'. The Psalms themselves are intended to be Torah, understood as teaching, or 'covenant-instruction'.

This is the almost unique flavour of the Psalms: that what was originally offered to God, is now given back to us as revelation from God. In other words, the Psalms are intended both to tell us something true about God and to show us appropriate ways of responding to God. That this happened was almost certainly the result of liturgical practice. Songs, hymns and prayers that were once offered to God by individual believers, like the king, or groups like the Levitical singers, are later incorporated into the Temple worship of Israel and in due course become God's prescription for how he might be praised and petitioned.

So Psalm 1 shows that the way in to the appreciation of the Psalms is to view them as Scripture – where we learn the will and works and ways of the Lord and, at the same time, learn how to respond to Him in righteous living and honest praise and prayer. In other words, as McCann says, 'Regardless of the fact that the Psalms originated as the response of the faithful persons to God, they are now to be understood also as God's word to the faithful.'[20]

This point is emphasised by the fivefold division of the book as we mentioned earlier (ie Psalms 2–41; 42–72; 73–89; 90–106; 107–150). This seems quite deliberately to match the fivefold division of the Pentateuch so that the Psalm collection represents a Davidic Torah that corresponds to the Mosaic Torah. The repeated 'doxologies' at the end of each book collection sum-marise the worshipping response to the words, will and ways of Yahweh celebrated or invoked in the preceding collection.

Psalm 1 forces a decision on would-be worshippers. In Walter Brueggemann's words, 'Human life is not mocked or trivialised. How it is lived is decisive.' The choice of being open or closed to God's 'Torah' is set before us and is the difference between life and death. There is no neutral ground!

Psalms and kingship

The second thing we need to know – if our prayers and praise are to be meaningful – is that the God whom we address is sovereignly in charge of our destiny. We need reassurance about what really determines our lives, and shapes our future. Are we pawns on the chessboard of fate? Are we cannon fodder for the military hardware that governs our world? Are we units of consumption at the mercy of global capitalists? We need a larger vision of the world than we are offered daily by the news media. Is there news beyond the News?

Israel needed to be frequently reassured. After all, God had overruled the mighty Pharaoh and released them from slavery in Egypt. This was the grounding conviction of their view of the world. But ever since, they had been a political football, kicked around by the superpowers of the day – from the Assyrians, to the Babylonians and beyond. The Psalms themselves reflect the end of Israel's national existence in the Babylonian Exile, when loss of land, temple, and monarchy raises huge questions about whether God is able or willing to help His people.

It is our question still. Are our lives at the mercy of dictators, warlords, politicians, global industrialists? Do they finally determine our lives? Or can we appeal to a higher authority?

Psalm 2 prophetically and decisively answers this question. It shows us the throne above all thrones, the King of all kings, the voice raised over all voices. Our God is sovereign over all things. To praise Him is common sense. History is going His way. He overrules the affairs of nations. He has already determined who will run His world. He has installed His King on His holy hill in Zion. This is a scandal and offence to the big shots in their summit conferences, for this hill is nowhere near the highest hill and doesn't even figure in their political topography. But it is a holy hill, the most strategic point, where heaven's rule and earth's rebellion are on collision course to meet. On this holy and unholy hill one day the battle-lines will converge and God and His rebellious creatures will find themselves at cross-purposes at the final showdown.

Meanwhile, it was Israel's conviction that their God was no mere tribal or national God but was in fact the One Creator God, the Lord of the nations. Psalm 2 opens the door to confident praise and meaningful prayer because it confirms in dramatic fashion that the God we worship is in charge of the affairs of the whole earth.

So Psalm 2 celebrates the kingship of God – the Lord reigns. It raises and offers an answer to the key question behind everything that goes on in our world: who rules the world?

In line with the suzerain–vassal (or 'sovereign–subject') treaty's typical stance, the book affirms the absoluteness of the covenant Lord's authority and the expected response of His willing and grateful subjects. 'And it is this theme of the reign of God which is the integrating centre of the theology of the entire book. All else is in one way or another connected to and dependent on this divine sovereignty.'[21]

The Lord's kingship is represented by:
(a) a place: Zion (Jerusalem), the City of the Great King, eg Psalms 46, 48, and
(b) a person: His chosen and anointed king.

Just like His Torah, God's sovereignty is contested by opposition. The 'righteous' who relish God's law and will are opposed by 'the wicked' who rebel against God's will and ways. Similarly, in Psalm 2, the rebellious 'kings' set themselves against God's kingship and 'his Anointed One' who embodies that kingship.

Psalm 2 heads a collection that praises the success of kingship in Israel (2–72) but is followed by a collection (73–89) which shows growing disenchantment with kings until the pivotal psalm – Psalm 89 – is reached. This is a long lament over the promise and subsequent failure of the Davidic kings and questions the future of the Davidic Covenant. Psalms 90–100 decisively answer this problem by celebrating the kingship of Yahweh itself as that which pre-dates, transcends and supersedes all delegated rule in Israel. Psalms 93–99 ring with the affirmation that 'The LORD reigns … the LORD is King …' – a confidence reborn in the trauma of exile and the loss of land, temple, and monarchy.

Psalm 2 from the outset encourages us to see the whole notion of kingship eschatologically and messianically. That is, don't look for an intermediate form of kingship but pin your hope on the ultimate form of kingship coming from the future. Frankly, if we do not in the end read the kingship Psalms messianically and Christologically, I see little reason for reading them at all.

Taken as a pair, Psalms 1 and 2 offer the 'invitation to be open to God's instruction and to the reality of God's reign in the world. Those who choose to live in covenant under God's rule will praise, pray, lament, believe and hope in God'.[22] They do this in the confidence that only God's kingdom lasts and that only God's future is worth waiting for. Comparing the details of each text can further highlight the shared function of the two psalms.

The tree and the throne

The Psalm collection encompasses both intensely personal piety (as in Psalm 1) and the turbulence of international politics (as in Psalm 2). God's blessing is bestowed in each realm on those who show covenant faith and faithfulness:

- 'Blessed is the man who does not walk in the counsel of the wicked ... ' (1:1)
- 'Blessed are all who take refuge in him.' (2:12)

The picture of the righteous person in Psalm 1 is writ large in the figure of God's anointed king in Psalm 2. The righteous man exists apart from the counsel of the wicked, just as the king is set apart from the conspiracies of the rebellious rulers of the earth.

Walking, standing, sitting – this is what we do all the time, it is the stuff of everyday living. Covenant integrity is measured by the moral choices we make every day as to the advice we heed, the aims and attitudes we adopt, even the company we keep. So God's king rules, as God's regent, amidst a raging world of rival powers, competing factions, and clashing truth claims.

Whether sitting in hotel lounges, business meetings, or summit conferences, participants in the human drama face the same challenge. The same verb used for 'meditating' (1:2) is used in Psalm 2:1 for 'plotting'; both righteous and wicked take a stance towards God's law. One delights in it; the others mock it.

It is worth saying again that the law of the Lord – 'Torah' – is here to be understood not in the restrictive sense of commandments, but in the richer sense of God's 'instruction', the covenant charter by which Israel was intended to live. To be sure this includes laws in the imperative sense, which say: 'You shall' and 'You shall not', but it also includes the foundational stories that define the redeemed and chosen people of God and that say 'You are ...' and 'You may become'.

This is the reservoir of truth – roughly equivalent at the very least to the first five books of the Bible – which the psalmist envisages the righteous man being sourced by. To the wicked, however, both at the domestic and political level, God's Torah is not a resource to live by but a restraint that must be cast off if life is to be lived (2:3). Ironically and tragically, the very Torah, which centres on the redemptive Exodus story by which God makes us free, is misconstrued by sinners as that which inhibits human freedom!

But to be truly free is to live the God-given, God-determined, God-shaped life. So the righteous man is like a tree planted, grounded in the truly human life, and the king is 'installed on God's holy hill', re-established in the truly human royal vocation. The contrast in both cases is sharp between the established tree and secure kingship and the frantic toing and froing of the wicked or the frenetic posturing of the renegade rulers.

But this is not a simple opposition of the active to the contemplative life. What is being compared here is not life in the fast lane with those who prefer the winding pathway of spiritual sightseeing. The question is: what are we absorbed by? What are we meditating on, chewing, on, ruminating on, drawing on, responding to?[23]

The righteous man is sourced by God's revelation, draws from the wells of salvation, taps into the reservoir of truth, quenches his thirst with the life-giving water of God's inscripturated Word. This echoes Joshua's rallying call to the generation on the verge of the promised land: 'Do not let this Book of the Law depart from your mouth; meditate on it day and night, so that you may be careful to do everything written in it. Then you will be prosperous and successful' (Josh. 1:8).

Psalm 2 corresponds with this in its portrayal of God's anointed king drawing all his inspiration from the words God had spoken to him (cf. Deut. 17:18–20). In particular, the king in Israel can apply to himself the specific promises made to the Davidic line of kings and say: 'I will proclaim the decree of the LORD ...' (Psa. 2:7a). That word or 'decree' is the covenant of kingship first made with David by which the king in Jerusalem is addressed as God's 'son' and can call on God as Father (2:7. cf. 2 Sam. 7:14).

In stark contrast to the rebellious rulers of the earth who seek to run God's world without Him, the true King is glad to allow His identity and destiny to be shaped by God's own covenant promise.

We may be among those who rack up air miles, fly business class to the wings of the morning, manipulate global markets and oversee international affairs. Or we may seldom stray from our village. In either case the issue posed by the Psalms is not how far have you travelled but how deeply have you lived? Are you a God-planted tree? Do your roots touch living water?

In Clinton McCann's words,

> The righteous have a place to be grounded, to take root, to be nourished, and to grow. They 'prosper' not in acquiring wealth and fame but in having somewhere to stand as a sure foundation. For the psalmist that foundation is to delight in, and meditate on,

'torah', to be constantly open to instruction. Taking such a stand or such a stance enables one to live with purpose and integrity in a world of confusion. It enables one to live with hope in a world of despair, and it enables one to perceive the mystery of life where others may perceive only the misery of life.[24]

And trees are known by the fruit they bear. The people who delight in God's Word, meditate on it, and draw deeply from it, become fruitful and productive. They prosper – not in some crass get-rich-quick fashion – but in fulfilling the potential placed within them. Similarly, on the political scale, the King who lives out the messianic destiny will bear fruit like a tree whose branches cover the world, to whom all nations bow as His inheritance, and the ends of the earth as His possession! This is the secret of the unwithered life on the one hand, and the unending kingdom on the other. The fate of the wicked is to be chaff blown away on the wind (1:4) or discarded as shards of broken pottery (2:9).

Our moral choices matter and have ultimate consequences. The two ways diverge and reach polar opposite destinations. The way of rebellion leads to perishing and destruction (1:6; 2:12); the way of the Lord is overseen by providential grace and leads home to the final refuge of God's kingship (1:6; 2:12b). Blessed is the person who walks the way of God's Word and arrives at the blessedness of the final kingdom.

Two key metaphors – the pathway and the refuge

The two key metaphors which emerge from the first two psalms are 'path' and 'refuge'. They encapsulate the dynamic interplay we experience, between movement and stability. Usually, we find this stimulating; sometimes we find it stressful. But we can never escape the challenge of holding together what is fluid and what is flexible, what changes and what is permanent. There is movement and adventure and risk in an open future. There is a refuge to be rushed to, and a refuge to be reached. In this way the two psalms set the tone for the rest of the collection as it traverses the extremes of human experience. And so the two psalms and their key metaphors reflect the interaction in our lives between what is fixed and what is in flux.

The way of the Lord

The righteous – those in covenant partnership with God – are people on the move. They have a sense of direction and purpose. There is meaning to their lives. God's Word – His Torah – maps out the way of the Lord and is a light to our path (Psa. 119:105). We respond by walking in His ways, not merely as a matter of outward observance, but as the delight of the heart. This moral conduct can be taught so that the heart remains focused and undivided (Psa. 86:11).

The path is not a headlong dash but a winding trail, not a sprint but a marathon. On this journey it is vital to stop – not just to stand and stare – but to meditate and take to heart. This is the way of covenant (Psa. 44:17–18), the paths of righteousness (Psa. 23:3), the very pathway of life itself (Psa. 16:11). The metaphor of a path sets us up on a journey through the whole Psalm collection as we accompany the psalmist through the landscape of life. Along the way we feel his joys and fears, failures and triumphs, pain and doubt, guilt and grace, despair and hope.

Pilgrimage is at the heart of the whole movement. Precisely because we travel on God's route in search of God's refuge we are pilgrims not aimless wanderers: 'Through many dangers, toils and snares, I have already come. 'Tis grace that brought me safe thus far, and grace will lead me home' (John Newton).

Psalm 23, for example, is far from the simple, pastoral idyll it is often taken to be. It tells the harrowing tale of a pilgrim harassed by enemies and shadowed by death, who is nonetheless guided and protected by the Lord his Shepherd.

Cries for help, God's saving intrusions, the commitments and claims of God's covenant-love, the moral obligations of holiness, the instruction in the ways of the Lord – all these form the fabric of the Psalms. Journeys through guilt to forgiveness, through doubt to deeper trust, through anger to peace, the agony of exile, and the rest of arrival in God's sanctuary and homecoming to God's kingdom – these are the life narratives the Psalms tell. They are a veritable tapestry of Israel's richly textured history. The psalmist's life narrative mirrors the life story of God's people. 'Through the "pathway" metaphor the individual is construed as Israel in miniature and vice-versa.'[25]

The historical Psalms in which Israel's own memories of grace form a litany of praise are not just patriotic flag-waving. They form the indispensable overarching framework in which the individual Israelite can locate his or her position on the journey. An individual worshipper can read his or her own story as interwoven with the national narrative and find hope and direction. 'History is the arena in which the Israel of the past and the Israelite in the present join their voice in common petition'[26] – and, we might add, in common praise.

The rule of God

If 'path' or 'way' is the key metaphor of Psalm 1, then 'refuge' is the key metaphor in Psalm 2.

- 'Blessed are all those who take refuge in him.' (2:12)

The 'refuge' is God's kingship and sovereignty, located in Zion and associated with the anointed king there. The 'refuge' more specifically is God's sanctuary, His dwelling-place where His restlessness has ended and His rest is established (Psa. 132:13–14). To arrive at His throne is to know the security of His loving kingship, the stability of His kingdom, the holiness of His Temple, and the peace of his rest. Paradoxically, this is not merely a goal that lies ahead of us in the dim distant future. It can be entered into now by faith. In fact that is just what faith for the journey consists of. 'To seek refuge in God is to place one's trust fully in God rather than in any self-procured means of security.'[27]

Such trust is not just the prize at the end of the journey but the prerequisite of starting out! Already the pilgrim takes refuge in God as the only empowerment for the long road ahead. This is precisely the challenge set before us. God's way may be the 'way less travelled' and narrower than others but it leads to a fulfilled life in God's kingdom.

But to opt for this road, and to decide to take shelter in God is a moral choice. The road we choose to travel on shapes our ethics. Our moral character is formed largely by the direction our life is turned in and by the destination inscribed on our heart. Equally, our behaviour and attitudes are defined by the choice of habitation. The ungodly man 'did not make God his stronghold' (Psa. 52:7). Our conduct is inevitably governed by our source of security.[28]

King and refuge share the same territory. God is our refuge and strength and to take refuge in Him is what faith does. It is God's royal role, and that of His appointed King, to make the world a saved and safer place, and to provide refuge and protection especially for the most vulnerable. 'God's "path" and God's "refuge" therefore signal the two complementary poles of divine activity: God's movement and God's indwelling, God's advent and God's enthronement, a dynamic sometimes, elusive presence.'[29]

Of course, just as there is *stability* alongside movement in Psalm 1 – the tree planted firm beside water as well as the pathway – so there is *movement* in Psalm 2. The movement is the unfolding drama of God's kingdom in a world unwilling to align itself with

God's rule. The prophetic psalmist tracks the moves the nations make and charts the saving decrees and actions of God. To take refuge in such a God is not to be clutched suffocatingly to a warm bosom but to be caught up in an ongoing and scary drama in which God is the chief actor. It is vital to remember this if 'refuge' is not to become a fatal presumption. Jeremiah poured prophetic scorn on those who had turned this saving significance of Zion into a comfort-zone for self-indulgence (Jer. 7). He accused his contemporaries of making God's earthly address in the Temple an insurance policy against their being held accountable by God. So the prophet punctured the lazy trust in the inviolability of Zion, come what may. Instead he reminded the complacent of their calling to be God's pilgrim people, walking in His ways of covenant faithfulness. Otherwise, he warned, those taking easy refuge would become early refugees – and so, sadly, they did!

So Psalm 2 does two things: it envisages God's current rule as our only reliable security and, at the same time, holds out the prospect of God's coming to reign to bring justice and peace. This is what the later kingship Psalms point us to. For the movements that need to be made are not all ours, so that we take refuge now in His royal rule and then set our feet towards His future kingdom. The movement, thankfully, is God's too; in fact pre-eminently His. As He has come in Israel's past gloriously to save and redeem, to judge and make covenant, so we may look forward to this same God coming.

- The Lord reigns.
- The Lord comes.
- The Lord shows us the way.
- The Lord leads the way and is the way.

These twin images – pathway and refuge – then provide two powerful lenses through which to view the whole Psalm collection 'as a pilgrimage of prayer and sanctuary of praise'.[30]

'Refuge' is the direction or goal to which the 'path' leads and is at the same time the environment and climate in which the traveller is nourished on the journey.

'Pathway' gives to 'refuge' a sense of movement, that prevents us becoming passive. It challenges us to a daring obedience and entices us with the promise of an exciting discovery. It ensures that taking refuge in God and dwelling under His wings remains a morally stimulating and spiritually stretching experience.

'Refuge' creates space for freedom. Salvation here is to be brought into a 'broad' or 'large' space (see Psa. 18:19, 36; 31:8; 119:45). So the psalmist's 'pathway' is widened into a 'refuge'.[31] Room is made by redemption not only for security but also for freedom and growth and community. Nor is this a ghetto existence, an introverted, holy huddle of self-indulgent praisers. It is a refuge that gives boldness to witness to the world and to call on all nations to give God glory.

'Pathway' says William Brown, is the 'ongoing process of refuge-making by which the psalmist can ultimately leave behind the cry for vengeance in favour of the call to praise, a move illustrated by the movement of the Psalter as a whole'.[32] This movement passes through lament and imprecation until it arrives at the sunlit uplands of universal acclamation of the One Creator God (Psa. 145–150). In other words, our final refuge and destination is the praise of all creation in a cosmic sanctuary.

On the pathway we enjoy His refuge. In His refuge we press on for the prize of the upward call of God. We join our battle-scarred lives to the turbulent history told in the Psalms; we in our turn are incorporated into the covenantal narrative of God's people. We climb its mountains of revelation and vantage; we plumb its depths of despair and powerlessness; we trudge its shadowed valleys of sorrow and arid wildernesses of exile. We recoil at its cutting crises and endure its wrenching transitions. We echo its cries, pray its prayers, and blend our songs with the chorus of praise. We lift up our hearts and our eyes to the coming kingdom. Secure despite all, we press on along the pilgrim way.

The paradox of the fixed and the flexible, the moving and the settled, point us to the metaphors I have used – the four seasons. It is precisely the changing seasons, which are a pledge of God's unchanging faithfulness to His created order: 'As long as the earth endures, seedtime and harvest, cold and heat, summer and winter, day and night will never cease' (Gen. 8:22).

SUMMER SONGS

PSALMS

'... summertime, and the living is easy ...'

- Summer songs are hymns of praise, pure and simple.
- They grab our attention by their exuberant praise of God.
- In them God is acclaimed with unbounded enthusiasm.
- God's excellence is celebrated.
- God's many-splendoured qualities are relished.
- The redeemed rejoice in God's saving deeds.

In these hymns you will hear festive music: fierce shouts of joy, and jubilant song, intermingling with invigorating trumpet blasts and the evocative wail of rams' horns, and all done with every stop pulled out! Psalms 100, 103, 136, 146–150 are sample psalms. No hint of trouble, or memory of disorder mars the melody. All dissonance has long since been resolved in confident trust.

The basic structure of such songs is illustrated at its simplest in Psalm 117, a summons to praise: 'Praise the LORD all you nations; extol him, all you peoples'; the reasons for praise: 'For great is his love towards us, and the faithfulness of the LORD endures for ever'; a renewed summons to praise: 'Praise the LORD'.

All modern psalm research is indebted to the work of Claus Westermann. He classified all psalms of praise into two categories. The first he termed descriptive praise – that is, praising God for what He is and characteristically does. The second he called declarative praise, which praises God for His unique, saving intervention usually in response to a specific prayer for help.[33] We will reserve consideration of this type of song for a later section.

What I have termed 'summer songs' denotes those songs of descriptive praise that celebrate God's attributes and activity.

Psalm 145 is a complete example of such a song. The psalmist praises God as great, good, majestic, righteous, compassionate, glorious, faithful, loving. He commits himself to lifelong praise and calls on 'every creature' to praise God's holy name. God's 'name' is the centrepiece of Israel's praise since it is His 'name'

(Yahweh) which sums up all the revealed truth of all that God is and does for His people, so Psalm 99:3: 'Let them praise your great and awesome name – he is holy.'

God's name is unique and so the hymns of praise contrast God to idols, for example Psalm 96:5, 'God is to be feared above all gods, for the gods of the nations are idols.'

These songs correspond to the Hebrew verb *halal* from which the repeated call to 'praise the LORD' ('hallelujah') derives (see especially Psa. 146–150). The word conveys the thought of 'publicly acknowledging', even 'being excitedly boastful', about something or someone. Because such songs catch the eye and provide the climax to the collection, the Psalms are called in Hebrew *tehillim* ('praises').

In terms of emotional mood, 'summer songs' are usually serene and untroubled. The praise is pure and direct and exuberant. The worshippers seem undistracted by their own condition. The focus is on God and His goodness. Such psalms reflect that life is going well: God is in His heaven and all is right with the world. Thank God there are such times. We rejoice to live – at least for short periods of our lives – under unclouded skies. Praise at these times delights in God's generosity and blessings. Songs of praise put on record the unchanging certainties that sustain our existence with God. They admire and relish God's special qualities and attributes, not least His wisdom and energy as the One Creator God. They acclaim God as the covenant Lord of His people and revel in the bond of love that ties Him to His people.

Consider the following five features of 'hymns of praise'.

1. Praising God in the Psalms has its reasons
- Summon an international chorus:
  'Praise the LORD, all you nations ... For great is his love towards us ...' (Psa. 117:1)

42

- Stir God's own people:
  '... *praise his name. For the* LORD *is good and his love endures for ever* ...' (Psa. 100:4–5)

- Make personal confession:
  '*I love the* LORD, *for he heard my voice; he heard my cry for mercy*' (Psa. 116:1)

In each case it is made clear what is the ground of praise: namely, the character and saving mercy of God. There is a passionate, theological logic to Israel's praise. It is neither mindless, nor meaningless nor contentless. It is praise with good reason.

2. Praising God in the Psalms is the appropriate response to who God is and who we are

God is the Covenant Lord and we are His people. 'Know that the LORD is God. It is he who made us, and we are his; we are his people, the sheep of his pasture' (Psa 100:3). Worshipping God is the fitting way to acknowledge who He is as Lord and who we are as His flock. Praise celebrates a covenantal relationship. Given the nature of the case, such praise is inevitable. As Mount Everest is there to be climbed and a Rembrandt painting to be admired, so God by His very nature is there to be worshipped. In other words, 'Great is the LORD, and most worthy of praise' (Psa. 48:1).

3. Praising God in the Psalms engages the whole of human personality

Praise is what we were made for. Praise is our *raison d'être*, our very reason for living. To turn away from the praise of the One Creator God is to dehumanise ourselves, so that we opt for an idolatrous substitute or settle into a narcissistic self-love. We diminish ourselves by withholding praise from God. But when we worship, we find ourselves 'at full stretch before God'.[34]

Praise in the Psalms is the offering of the whole self to God in grateful response for His covenant mercy and grace.

One psalmist press-gangs all his inner powers to worship the Lord and lays urgent siege to capture his own soul for the praise of God: 'Let all that is within me praise his holy name.' Praise is breath-taking, 'a matter of life and breath'.[35] So, in Claus Westermann's words, 'Where there is life there is praise.'[36] Or as Clinton McCann puts it, 'The goal of human life is praise.'[37]

4. Praising God in the Psalms is the goal of the whole creation

The summons to the self to praise becomes a call to the Church and, in turn, issues a universal invitation: 'Let everything that has breath praise the LORD' (Psa. 150:6).

But nature is inarticulate, its speech is soundless (Psa. 19). It is part of our unique human privilege to be, in George Herbert's words, 'the world's high priest' who 'doth present the sacrifice for all'. As worshippers, we act, as it were, in a secretarial capacity, putting words to creation's praise.

> Of all the creatures both in sea and land,
> Only to man Thou hast made known Thy ways,
> And put the pen alone into his hand
> And made him secretarie of Thy praise.[38]

The final group of songs – Psalms 145–150, each of which ends with 'hallelujah' – 'Praise the LORD' – constitute an intentional crescendo to the entire collection. Though laments literally outnumber songs of praise and thanksgiving, there is a quite deliberate movement in the collection which takes us beyond lament and culminates in universal rejoicing in the One Creator God. Final resolution will be achieved with ultimate redemption when everything in the cosmos is reconciled to the one will that made it and reunited with the one love that created it. 'As one moves through the sanctuary of the Psalter, hymns of praise turn into veritable praise choruses while laments die away.'[39]

5. Praising God in the Psalms blesses God!

The ability to bless God is a remarkable feature of Old Testament piety and practice, later followed in the classic Jewish tradition in the great prayers which begin 'Berakah ...', 'Blessed be ...'. The Old Testament highlights such prayers (1 Chron. 16:36; 29:10, 20; 1 Kings 8:15) and the Psalms also illustrate them (eg, Psa. 34; 103).

Because this is now familiar to us, we may miss how extraordinary this kind of prayer is. It leads Brueggemann to call praise an 'audacious act'. Why?

You see, it's difficult at first to envisage how our praise can possibly bring blessing to God. Does God lack something that He needs supplementing by us? Does praise make up some deficiency in God?

Perhaps, as Gerald Wilson suggests, it was this misgiving that gave the initial translators of the NIV cold feet, and caused them to substitute 'praise' for 'bless' in every case.[40]

It is a pity the NIV translators were timid here. As a result we miss, in translation, the direct linkage between God blessing us and our blessing God. This carries over into the New Testament, again with the unhelpful loss of a key connection between God's action and our response (see Eph. 1:3ff; 1 Pet. 1:3ff).

Wilson usefully articulates a way out of any perceived problem. 'While it may be theologically correct to say that God is unchanged by our blessing or cursing, it is certainly true that when his creation returns divine blessing, his purposes are brought to completion in a way that is not possible without that response'.[41]

The psalmist is unabashed. 'I will bless the LORD at all times; His praise shall continually be in my mouth ... O magnify the LORD with me, And let us exalt His name together' (Psa. 34:1, 3 NASB). We are used to God blessing us and we thank and love Him for all the blessings we have received. But this psalm is a ringing endorsement of the fact that here in praise, as Walter Brueggemann has it, 'the traffic runs "upstream" as the speaker acts upon God'.[42]

So how can we 'bless' God and 'perfect perfection'? Psalm 34 perhaps offers us a clue when it invites us to bless, magnify or glorify (NIV) God together.

- To bless is to bestow the power for life.
- To magnify is to make large, great, and more significant.
- To glorify is to make heavy, prominent, and weighty.

Can we enrich God in any way?
Can we by praising increase his stature?
We must answer 'no' and yet these terms are startling.

In his typically bold way, Walter Brueggemann suggests that 'praise bestows something upon Yahweh, as though Yahweh needed or desired or at least received something God does not yet have'.[43]

No wonder praise is an 'audacious act'. Maybe it is in our perception of Him that God is enhanced or enriched. Perhaps the corporate dynamic of worship in Psalm 34 is the only 'psychological' answer we can give, in that by coming together in worship a magnification of God occurs. In worship, God, as it were, looms larger, draws closer, and appears clearer.

- God looms larger, so that 'those who fear him' discover that God dwarfs all other fears (vv. 4–14).
- God draws closer to the downcast so that in close-up view of God (we notice His eyes and face and ears) He is found to be 'near to the brokenhearted' (vv. 15–18).
- He comes into sharper focus for the afflicted who see more clearly than ever before that He is their God and on their side (vv. 19–22).

Whatever else it does 'blessing' gathers up into one the response of a grateful people and creation, and offers it back 'with interest' to the God who gave so lavishly. 'Gratitude is that which completes the circle whereby blessing returns to the Giver in the form of unending adoration' (William Hendrickson).

Daniel Hardy and David Ford put it well: 'Blessing is the comprehensive praise and thanks that returns all reality to God, and so lets all be taken up into the spiral of mutual appreciation and delight which is the fulfilment of creation.'[44]

Hardy and Ford call this 'the ecology of blessing'.[45]

In this ecosystem of love, the life of God is maintained: it is this love – flowing out of Him to us and back to Him again in loving praise and worship – which makes the world go round!

Garment of Praise (Psalm 33)

[1]Sing joyfully to the LORD, you righteous;
 it is fitting for the upright to praise him.
[2]Praise the LORD with the harp;
 make music to him on the ten-stringed lyre.
[3]Sing to him a new song;
 play skilfully, and shout for joy.

[4]For the word of the LORD is right and true;
 he is faithful in all he does.
[5]The LORD loves righteousness and justice;
 the earth is full of his unfailing love.

[6]By the word of the LORD were the heavens made,
 their starry host by the breath of his mouth.
[7]He gathers the waters of the sea into jars;
 he puts the deep into storehouses.
[8]Let all the earth fear the LORD;
 let all the people of the world revere him.
[9]For he spoke, and it came to be;
 he commanded, and it stood firm.

[10]The LORD foils the plans of the nations;
    he thwarts the purposes of the peoples.
[11]But the plans of the LORD stand firm for ever,
    the purposes of his heart through all generations.

[12]Blessed is the nation whose God is the LORD,
    the people he chose for his inheritance.
[13]From heaven the LORD looks down
    and sees all mankind;
[14]from his dwelling-place he watches
    all who live on earth –
[15]he who forms the hearts of all,
    who considers everything they do.
[16]No king is saved by the size of his army;
    no warrior escapes by his great strength.
[17]A horse is a vain hope for deliverance;
    despite all its great strength it cannot save.
[18]But the eyes of the LORD are on those who fear him,
    on those whose hope is in his unfailing love,
[19]to deliver them from death
    and keep them alive in famine.

[20]We wait in hope for the LORD;
    he is our help and our shield.
[21]In him our hearts rejoice,
    for we trust in his holy name.
[22]May your unfailing love rest upon us, O LORD,
    even as we put our hope in you.

SOMETIMES THE KEY FITS THE LOCK PERFECTLY. YOU
know the moment.

You are shopping for new clothes. She comes out of the changing
room, resplendent in the new dress she needs for the wedding!

You sigh with relief: 'Splendid … it suits you … you look great!

That shade looks good on you ... the cut is just right ... very flattering ... what a good fit ... comfortable too ... very becoming.' And all the ingredients come together: colour, style, fashion, function and comfort; a perfect fit in every way. In other words – the key fits the lock.

And so it is with praise. Just as certain people look best in the Armani suit or Versace frock or Levi jeans, so everyone sounds their best when praising God! 'It is fitting for the upright to praise him' (v.1).

Praise is 'fitting' because all the elements come together as if they were meant to be together (v.2): heartfelt convictions of faith, God-given musical skill, the exuberant emotions of joy released from feeling and responding to God's love ... and a cascade of songs and hymns.

Praise: it's the key that fits your lock; praise is the garment that becomes you.

Time and again another great excuse presents itself for a 'new song' (v.3). Fresh victories of grace, fresh visions of God inspire a flood of new melodies and new songs.

Why? Because there are good reasons for praise.

(a) Let us celebrate 'the word of the LORD ...' (vv.4-9)

Firstly, praise God for His covenant word. The word of covenant promise introduces Israel to all the classic language by which God is described in relationship to His people. These are the terms Israel had learned to relish since God redeemed them and entered into covenant with them. As Liberator and Covenant-maker, God had demonstrated His integrity, shown that His words were matched by His deeds, that He does what He says. So praise is due for His trustworthiness. God is 'true ... faithful ... righteousness'. 'He loves justice.' Above all, sing joyfully to the Lord for the 'earth is full of his unfailing love'. This passionate commitment, this '*hesed*' is God's trademark. '*Hesed*', the nearly untranslatable term, is the nearest equivalent to the New Testament concept of grace. '*Hesed*'

– God's strong, enduring, covenant-love!

This word speaks promise and commitment – 'I love you … you are my special people … I will be with you … be your God and you will be my people …'. Israel exemplifies a people who do not live by bread alone but by every word of unfailing love that comes from God's mouth. Patriarchs and prophets, kings and psalmists, priests and sages – all sing the new song of praise from the same song sheet.

Secondly, praise God for His creative word (vv.6–8). In the beginning, we read in Genesis, His 'let there be … and there was'. In the Old Testament view of the world, God's word not only informs but also acts. It comes freighted with creative power. God's word is powerful, an energetic partner of His life-giving 'breath' or Spirit.

So the prophet heralds the dynamic word of God that accomplishes the purpose for which God sends it forth (Isa. 55:10–11). For this God commands universal respect and evokes the 'awe' of the whole world (vv.8–9).

(b) Let us celebrate 'the plans of the LORD' which 'stand firm …' (vv.10–12)

It is a matter of praise that God 'foils the plans of the nations' (vv.10–11). Israel owed its existence to God's overruling wisdom. The Egyptian Pharaoh's plans to hold on to the enslaved Israelites were countermanded by God's 'Let my people go …'.

During World War II, the Allies confused the German High Command in occupied France as to where the invasion of Europe would begin. In a subterfuge dubbed, 'The man who never was', the body of an unknown man was fitted out as a naval officer with a set of phony invasion plans to fool the enemy. So God's paradoxical subterfuge subverts the strategies of the international powers of the ancient world.

The besieging Assyrian armies succumb to a mysterious plague; the Babylonians become His own tool of judgment; the pagan

Persian warlord, Cyrus, becomes God's unwitting but anointed agent in freeing God's people from Babylonian captivity and to setting them on the way home. So God's strategy shapes history (Isa. 14:27; 46:10). It is a matter for great rejoicing for, 'Blessed is the nation whose God is the LORD, the people he chose for his inheritance' (v.12).

The company is taken over in a merger with a larger outfit. The new CEO calls you in, and you wonder if you're going to be involved in the new set-up. He offers you not only promotion but a partnership. And you feel satisfied that you're part of their plans. Israel's joy and praise in the strategy of God is ours too. Our greatest joy and happiness is to be part of God's plans! Jeremiah's pastoral comfort for the disconsolate exiles was that God had plans for them, plans to give them a future and a hope (Jer. 29:10–11).

(c) Let us celebrate 'the eyes of the LORD' (vv.13–19)
His watchful eyes miss nothing. Is this a threat? Some people feel it is. But if so, it is only a threat to those in rebellion against Him.

The tower of Babel (Gen. 11) – probably an ancient ziggurat or pyramid-type structure – was a symbol of a proud godless culture that wanted to leave no room for God. In the humour of the narrative, so presumptuous and pathetic is this humanistic attempt to reach up to the heights of heaven that God has to come down in order to inspect it! Now as the psalmist hymns it, God looks down (vv.16–17). What He sees is human powerplay. He reviews our pretentious May Day parades, inspects the whole panoply of militaristic swagger and military hardware – and He's not impressed.

Is God's all-seeing eye a comfort then? Surely, yes – to His people who trust Him.

I remember talking to a friend some years ago, who had been raised in a strict and forbidding Presbyterian home in northern Scotland. 'Thou God Seest Me' was the appliquéd message framed and hanging over your bed like the sword of Damocles. God was intending to spy on you and catch you out. He was the big nasty policeman in the sky. What a terribly distorted view of God that was, as someone out to get you even when you put the light out!

It's a dreadful slander on God. His eye is on His people but it is the eye of watchful care; His intense and loving interest in every detail of their lives. Which would you prefer: to be 'noticed' or 'overlooked'?

So praise overflows into prayer – prayer that is confident and hopeful about the future: 'We wait in hope for the LORD' (vv. 20–22).

The Lord is Lord over creation: summon the white-coated experts from ICI or Shell; summon Richard Dawkins and Bill Gates; summon the players of financial markets and global industrialists to: Praise the Lord.

He's the great Friend of the Earth; it's His world; He had the first word and He will have the last word on it all.

The Lord is Lord of the nations: command the grey-suited in Beijing, the Ayatollahs, the Democrats in Westminster and Congress, the bureaucrats in Brussels, the media-tycoons in Australia to – 'Praise the Lord.' The nations belong to Him; His plans shape history His way.

The Lord is Lord of people: call on doctors and psycho-therapists, and surgeons, and social workers and all who care for people to: Praise the Lord!

He made people, He knows what suits them best, He knows what's fit for them.

Of all that the psalmist celebrates, it is the 'unfailing love' of God that dominates his song (vv.5b, 18b, 22).

Praise for the love that fills the earth (v.5b) and that oversees His people's deliverance (v.18b).

Pray, confident that the power of love not the love of power will prevail.

'Love us God, with all you've got – that's what we're depending on.'
(v.22, *The Message*)

For love's sake, put on the 'garment of praise'.
It will suit you and never go out of fashion.

Theatre of Glory (Psalm 104)

[1]Praise the LORD, O my soul.

O LORD my God, you are very great;
    you are clothed with splendour and majesty.
[2]He wraps himself in light as with a garment;
    he stretches out the heavens like a tent
[3] and lays the beams of his upper chambers on their waters.
He makes the clouds his chariot
    and rides on the wings of the wind.
[4]He makes winds his messengers,
    flames of fire his servants.

[5]He set the earth on its foundations;
    it can never be moved.
[6]You covered it with the deep as with a garment;
    the waters stood above the mountains.
[7]But at your rebuke the waters fled,
    at the sound of your thunder they took to flight;
[8]they flowed over the mountains,
    they went down into the valleys,
    to the place you assigned for them.
[9]You set a boundary they cannot cross;
    never again will they cover the earth.

[10]He makes springs pour water into the ravines;
  it flows between the mountains.
[11]They give water to all the beasts of the field;
  the wild donkeys quench their thirst.
[12]The birds of the air nest by the waters;
  they sing among the branches.
[13]He waters the mountains from his upper chambers;
  the earth is satisfied by the fruit of his work.
[14]He makes grass grow for the cattle,
  and plants for man to cultivate –
  bringing forth food from the earth:
[15]wine that gladdens the heart of man,
  oil to make his face shine,
  and bread that sustains his heart.
[16]The trees of the LORD are well watered,
  the cedars of Lebanon that he planted.
[17]There the birds make their nests;
  the stork has its home in the pine trees.
[18]The high mountains belong to the wild goats;
  the crags are a refuge for the conies.

[19]The moon marks off the seasons,
  and the sun knows when to go down.
[20]You bring darkness, it becomes night,
  and all the beasts of the forest prowl.
[21]The lions roar for their prey
  and seek their food from God.
[22]The sun rises, and they steal away;
  they return and lie down in their dens.
[23]Then man goes out to his work,
  to his labour until evening.
[24]How many are your works, O LORD!
  In wisdom you made them all;
  the earth is full of your creatures.

²⁵There is the sea, vast and spacious,
   teeming with creatures beyond number –
   living things both large and small.
²⁶There the ships go to and fro,
   and the leviathan, which you formed to frolic there.

²⁷These all look to you
   to give them their food at the proper time.
²⁸When you give it to them,
   they gather it up;
when you open your hand,
   they are satisfied with good things.
²⁹When you hide your face,
   they are terrified;
when you take away their breath,
   they die and return to the dust.
³⁰When you send your Spirit,
   they are created,
   and you renew the face of the earth.

³¹May the glory of the LORD endure for ever;
   may the LORD rejoice in his works –
³²he who looks at the earth, and it trembles,
   who touches the mountains, and they smoke.

³³I will sing to the LORD all my life;
   I will sing praise to my God as long as I live.
³⁴May my meditation be pleasing to him,
   as I rejoice in the LORD.
³⁵But may sinners vanish from the earth
   and the wicked be no more.
Praise the LORD, O my soul.

Praise the LORD.

A FRIEND OF MINE, WHO IS AN OCEANOGRAPHER, WROTE to me some years ago from a research vessel in far northern waters. He told me of watching a satellite pass overhead in clear skies. 'On that same night', he went on, 'we saw the Aurora Borealis – very impressive. Being stuck on a small boat in the middle of the ocean and watching the Aurora makes you appreciate in a new way the grandeur of God's creation.'

'Contemporary people,' comments James Mays, 'have a variety of ways of viewing and speaking about the world and of what we moderns call "Nature"– scientific, economic, aesthetic, recreational ...'[46]

The scientific way brings the world to the laboratory where its global forces and energies are measured and calibrated by chemists, microbiologists, geologists, nuclear physicists, astronomers, ecologists, and explorers.

The economic way brings the world to the factory and assesses it for units of food production, yields per acre, and the search for the most efficient global markets.

The recreational way brings the world to the travel brochure or the video camera, and is interested in where holidays are spent, Bali or Bangkok, the Alps or the Swiss Lakes, the Grand Canyon.

The artistic way brings the world to the studio where painters and poets and photographers ponder its beauty like the great impressionists. My recommendation: forget the wrapping paper version, go and see the real thing – Monet's *Water Lilies* in L'Orangerie – in Paris!

But the psalmist, like my friend Meric, sees it all with the eyes of faith and bursts into song.

What moved him to praise? He looked at the world and saw it as if for the first time. Its beauty in form and function overwhelmed him. He gazed at the natural world with almost childlike awe, marvelling at the mystifying, multi-media, multi-sensory craftsmanship of God. He saw the world, in Calvin Seerveld's words, as the 'stunning theatre, workshop, playground of our

Father in heaven, peopled by whatever his creative word sustains'.[47]

The more prosaically minded might take interest in the rough correspondence between the psalm and the seven Genesis days of creation. So compare:

- Psalm 104:2-5 with Genesis 1:1-5;
- Psalm 104:6-9 with Genesis 1:6-8;
- Psalm 104:10-18 with Genesis 1:9-13;
- Psalm 104:19-23 with Genesis 1:14-19;
- Psalm 104:24-30 with Genesis 1:20-31;
- Psalm 104:31-35 with Genesis 2:23.

But it is poetry, not prose, that best enters into the spirit of this exuberant song and generates praise.

The vision of the created world as God's theatre, of course, stems from John Calvin. And in the psalm, creation bursts on us like the opening fanfare of a theatrical performance or cosmic fashion show with coats of many colours (vv.1-2). Or, if you choose to see it that way, it's a festive meal, a rattlingly-good party (vv.14-15), or a vast 'Sea World' where even dolphins have a whale of a time and whales play (v.26)!

In the psalm's dramatic opening stanza, God sweeps gloriously on to stage. Clothed majestically in a cloak of light – 'dressed in sunshine', as Peterson has it – God strides through the world, touching the dawn and sunset, riding the clouds of heaven, whipping up foam on the sea, soaring on up currents, bending the trees, kindling fire – and all with angelic assistants in his entourage (vv.1-4)!

In this glorious light, the psalmist sees light and rejoices over earth's *stability* (vv.5-9) for God imparts to His creation not only His vitality but also something of His own faithfulness and dependability. Despite violent storms the earth stands firm, the floodwaters are held back (v.5). Israel appreciated this, never being a nation of sea-lovers. For Israel the sea was emblematic of the threatening forces of chaos. It was good news to learn that God had fixed limits to prevent chaos returning. This was a reminder of His creative powers at the beginning and His redemptive mercy at the Flood.

The psalmist rejoices in the earth's *fruitfulness* (vv.10–18) for it is a well-watered garden, fertile and productive. There marauding lions find prey and labouring men find food. The psalmist paints a vivid picture of land teeming with life, rich and prolific. Gentle trout streams, rushing rivers, tall cedars, glistening cornfields, luxuriant grapevines, nesting storks and wild donkeys.

Throughout Israel's occupation of the Land of Promise, she was tempted to absorb features of the local Baalite religion. Baal, the Canaanite fertility god, threatened to usurp Yahweh's exclusive place of honour as the One Creator and Provider. Baalism was a modern-sounding mix of sexuality and consumerism which effectively encouraged a devotee to say: 'It was my own power that produced this' (see Hosea 2:8). We moderns are at an even greater distance from the source than the ancients. We need, as Israel needed, prophetic reminders, that the 'good land' is God's gift and that every perfect gift comes not from Wall Mart or Tesco but ultimately from His hand.

The psalmist praises God for the earth's *order and harmony* (vv.19–23) – springtime and harvest, night and day, morning and evening, sunrise and sunset. It has long been recognised that it is the regularity and consistency of the natural world that makes the observation or study of it possible.

This led to claims – often contested – that the roots of science have a biblical base. Certainly, it is hard to see how pure experimental science could have emerged except from within a broadly Judeo-Christian biblical view of the world. As the distinguished historian of science, Stanley Jaki, once observed, 'Science found its only viable birth within a cultural matrix permeated by a firm conviction about the mind's ability to find in the realm of things and persons a pointer to their Creator.'

Less well noticed among Christians perhaps, until recently, are the implications of the evident harmony in the created order. Somewhat belatedly but wisely, Christians too are now recognising the extraordinary inter-dependency of all living things and, as a result, are giving increased attention to environmental issues and ecological concerns.

The psalmist rejoices over the earth's *variety* (vv. 4–26), for the world is the fruit of God's multifaceted creativity and His many-splendoured wisdom. An infinite variety of life forms dazzle the observer. Never the same snowflake, dew on a spider's web, the smell of cut grass after rain, a dragonfly in sunlight.

Glory be to God for dappled things
For skies of couple-colour as a brinded cow,
For rose-moles all in stipple upon trout that swim.[48]

As Annie Dillard says, 'Look, in short, at practically anything – the coot's feet, the mantis's face, a banana, the human ear – and see that not only did the creator create everything, but that he is apt to create anything. He'll stop at nothing.'[49]

The psalmist rejoices over the earth's *renewal* (vv.27–30) which gives the lie to the sub-biblical idea of 'deism', the belief that God started the process, like a watchmaker assembling and winding a watch, but that He now remains aloof, allowing things to take their natural course.

No, the biblical doctrine of creation, sturdily affirmed by the psalmist, is not only that God created but that He sustains His creation by continuously pouring His life into what He has made.

If we ask, as indeed, in our careless exploitation of the earth, we should, whether the earth's precious resources will be exhausted. The answer is no: not if God gets His way. And He usually does. God is not subject to the law of entropy, nor need His creation be. The psalmist is neither sentimental – 'nature is red in tooth and claw' (v.21) – nor is he overly romantic; he is only too keenly aware that evil blights the picture (v.35). But he has confidence in the creative Spirit's renewing work.

As Gerard Manley Hopkins said, 'The world is charged with the grandeur of God.' And we hear the poet, and long to agree with him. Yet we know that it is easier to quote God's grandeur than to practise it. The underlying glory is trodden flat by the trampling feet of everyday concerns and is none too obvious. But we dare to believe, as Hopkins did, that 'there lives the dearest freshness deep down things'. It is audacious to believe this, but we do because when God sends forth His Spirit, He renews the face of the earth. We dare to trust that beyond the darkness, morning springs,

> Because the Holy Ghost over the bent World
> broods with warm breast and with ah!
> bright Wings. (*God's Grandeur*)

So our role in creation and our responsibilities in regard to it are affirmed:

- as *beneficiaries* (vv.14–15) – receive with thanks!
- as *stewards* (v.23) – rule and work with respect!
- as *observers* (v.24) – research with wonder!

and in all this

- as *worshippers* (vv.1,33) – rejoice by sharing God's own joy that what He has made is still 'very good' (v.31)!

However well or poorly we can see with the psalmist's eye or poet's vision, we too can pray for that same creative Spirit to brood over our work and play, our science and our art, and so raise a glimmer of glory even from the dust. And for all that we have already received, we can be truly thankful. For, in Annie Dillard's words, 'This ... is the extravagant landscape of the world, given,

given with pizzazz, given in good measure, pressed down, shaken together, and running over.'[50]

And when a shadow falls across this brilliant vision as it inevitably does, the long shadow of sin and evil and the blight on God's good creation, we can cry with the prophet Habbakuk: 'Though the fig-tree does not bud and there are no grapes on the vines … though there are no sheep in the pen and no cattle in the stalls, yet I will rejoice in the LORD, I will be joyful in God my Saviour' (Hab. 3:17–18).

Easter has given us a greater reach even than the anointed psalmist and inspired prophet, as the apostle Paul disclosed. When creation groans and crops fail and children are born crippled then we can fall back on the Lamb slain from before the creation of the world, fall back on to a salvation that is mysteriously deeper and older than the world itself, fall back into the everlasting arms of God underneath it all, a God who chose to create because He knew He had the power to redeem whatever creation should come to! And who, in the cross of His Son, did just that, reaffirming the goodness of His creation by raising Him from the dead, the firstfruits of a renewed world.

Songs of Impossibility (Psalm 146)

[1]Praise the LORD.

Praise the LORD, O my soul.
[2] I will praise the LORD all my life;
  I will sing praise to my God as long as I live.

[3]Do not put your trust in princes,
  in mortal men, who cannot save.
[4]When their spirit departs, they return to the ground;
  on that very day their plans come to nothing.

⁵Blessed is he whose help is the God of Jacob,
　　whose hope is in the LORD his God,
⁶the Maker of heaven and earth,
　　the sea, and everything in them –
　　the LORD, who remains faithful for ever.
⁷He upholds the cause of the oppressed
　　and gives food to the hungry.
The LORD sets prisoners free,
⁸　the LORD gives sight to the blind,
the LORD lifts up those who are bowed down,
　　the LORD loves the righteous.
⁹The LORD watches over the alien
　　and sustains the fatherless and the widow,
　　but he frustrates the ways of the wicked.

¹⁰The LORD reigns for ever,
　　your God, O Zion, for all generations.

Praise the LORD.

WE ARE UNUSUAL PEOPLE BECAUSE WE SPEND SO MUCH
time singing! Outside of choral societies, where else do people
regularly gather together to sing? Perhaps the office Christmas
party or the Rugby Club annual bash – but then only fuelled by
alcohol.

Yet the Bible shows us that when we are singing praises to
God we are doing the most natural thing in the world. When
we sing praises to God we are doing what human beings were
created to do.

Praise turns out to be our very reason for living. As we saw
earlier, in Ronald Allen's words: 'Praise is a matter of life and
breath.' Walter Brueggemann agrees: 'Praise is the duty and delight,
the ultimate vocation of the human community, indeed of all
creation. Yes, all of life is aimed toward God and finally exists for

the sake of God.'[51]

This is why the songbook of the Bible (the collection of the Psalms) climaxes with six choruses of 'hallelujah' – Psalms 146–150 – and this resounding 'praise the LORD' is an absolutely fitting finale! Every other kind of song in the Psalmody collection, representing every particular emotion and mood and crisis, is gathered up in the final burst of praise. The songs of desperate individuals, the exuberant thanksgiving of those who've been rescued, the searingly honest confessions of the guilty and forgiven, the national outpouring of lament and pain, the community's rejoicing over victory or harvest are all brought on stage for a last medley of praise. Everything in all creation destined for redemption is summoned to join in this boastful and excited praise of the Lord.

Old Testament scholar, Patrick Miller, says of praise: 'This is the last word of faith; the last sound in the universe.'[52]

Praise is faith set to music. This is why the psalm-singer quickly comes, in verses 3–4, to the issue of trust:

- Trust is damaged at an early age for most of us.
- Children are trusting until they get hurt.
- To trust is to be vulnerable.
- Loved ones let us down, friends betray us, the firm we've loyally served makes us redundant, the secrets we shared in confidence are gossiped around.

'Do not put your trust in princes' (v.3); they are mortals doomed to die. Impressive as they may appear to be, their power and prestige are like bubbles pricked by death. However high-profile, when their 'ruach' – their 'breath' or 'spirit' – departs, they deflate like punctured balloons.

So who can we trust? Well, not Jacob, for a start!

Jacob was a scoundrel, the original con man, not a man you would play cards with, or leave your house-keys with when you went on holiday. Jacob was not a man you'd buy a second-hand camel from! And those rugs and spices he's offering cheap … fell off the back of a caravan train … the Del Boy of the Near East.

Jacob cheated his brother Esau out of his birthright and then cheated him out of his blessing by deceiving their father Isaac (Gen. 25:27–34; 27:27, 35–36).

When the prophet Jeremiah wrote: 'do not trust your brothers. For every brother is a deceiver …' (Jer. 9:4), and when he said: 'the heart is deceitful above all things …', the word he used in Hebrew for 'deceiver' and 'deceitful' means 'Jacob-like' (Jer. 17:9). Jacob became a by-word for deception and double-dealing.

All the more remarkable then that God should be forever willing to be known as the God of Jacob.

'The God of *Abraham*' – I could understand that. 'The God of *Isaac*' – yes, that's feasible. But 'the God of *Jacob*' – that's astonishing!

But God made Himself known to this rascal, got hold of him, blessed him and reaffirmed the covenant promises to him which God had made with his father Isaac and grandfather Abraham! And God becomes the God of Abraham, Isaac, *and* Jacob.

What a God!!

How amazing that God is willing to be known as the 'God of Jacob'. This must be a God of amazing grace and mercy and love. If God can save and covenant with scallywags and con men like Jacob then there's hope for all of us. If God can turn slippery characters like Jacob into the founder of a nation Israel then He can make something even of you and me! No wonder He's worthy of so much praise!

Praise for God's works in creation (v.6)

Only if this is true can praise be possible.

If not then we have no one to thank but each other!

Praising the Creator reminds us that we are not self-sufficient, that all human management control is partial and limited, and that all our expertise is derived from God.

And the One Creator God 'remains faithful for ever' (v.6), committed as God is to His covenant, to creation, to everyone who trusts Him as their help and hope.

Praise for God's activity on behalf of the weak and needy (vv.7–9)

God is a God of justice on the side of the poor and marginalised, whose gracious option is for the oppressed, the hungry, the prisoners, the blind, and all persecuted righteous ones. For them wonders never cease. Their praise protests against all closed systems. Theirs are what Brueggemann calls 'songs of impossibility'.[53]

Abraham and Sarah, the barren ones, conceive, bear a child and share God's laughter in the birth of Isaac. Deborah, unlikely warrior woman, sings her song of victory. Hannah, the desperate Hannah, has a son and so 'God raises the poor ... and lifts the needy' (1 Sam. 2:8). Mary magnificently praises the God who has 'brought down rulers from their thrones but has lifted up the humble ... filled the hungry with good things but has sent the rich away empty' (Luke 1:52–53).

Because such 'songs of impossibility' express hope against all closed systems, it is not surprising that women are at the forefront of this chorus. So prison doors open, sight returns to the blind, the oppressed stand tall as burdens roll from their back, and wonders never cease. Praise rejoices in this social justice and revolutionary redemption!

The praise of Israel bore witness to transformations and reversals of condition too wonderful for any human capability to bring off on its own or even to comprehend. In such reversals, all human definitions of the way things have to be in this world are challenged and overturned.

The freedom and power of God say that is what is laughable from a human perspective is the way things are going to be when God is at work ... The doxologies of God's people are one of the fundamental indicators that wonders have not ceased.[54]

Our song is a 'song of impossibility' – a song of resurrection. We have a Prince who does not let us down, whose mortal flesh was cut down in its prime but who was raised from the dead, on whom the creative breath of God rests and remains as the last Adam, life-giving Spirit; He's our covenant Lord, fully worthy of our trust, well able to save.

Praise for the lasting kingdom

The Lord of the impossible 'reigns for ever' (v.10).

I feel sorry for politicians; their job is too minor and their manifestos too meagre compared to the gospel we proclaim. Any ordinary Christian – faithful, joyful, humble – has a bigger story to tell, a better citizenship to discharge, a greater kingdom to serve. As for dreams of the great or good society, an all-giving society, God's prophets got there first a long time ago.

When the Pope met Bob Dylan at a Catholic Youth festival, he characteristically remarked: 'You say "the answer, my friend, is blowing in the wind"; so it is but it is not the wind that blows things away; it is the wind that is the breath and life of the Holy Spirit. You ask me "how many roads must a man walk down before he becomes a man?" I answer: one! There is only one road for man, and it is the road of Jesus Christ who said – I am the Way and the Life.'

'Praise the LORD'!

Prayer and Reflections

I praise You for Your Word.

Your Word is truth, Your Word is mighty, Your Word speaks worlds into being and new life into my soul. Your Word is Jesus.

Help me to live by every word that comes from Your mouth.

I praise You for Your plans.

Your plans are mysterious and Your ways past finding out. Your strategy is sovereign and Your purpose sure to bring salvation.

I thank You that I do not have to have everything under my control but can trust that You do. Help me to live in confidence and faith that the Holy Spirit is wisely leading me even when I'm not sure what is going on.

I praise You for Your mercy.

Your mercy is lavish and steadfast. It cleanses, forgives and sustains me in a guilt-free joy. Your saving love endures forever, as firm as Your covenant.

Help me not to presume on Your grace but to act justly, to love mercy and to walk humbly with You, my God.

Eternity is too short to do justice to our praise of You, O Lord.

May my praise today join the universal chorus of all who call on Your name,

Hallelujah, Amen.

- With a Christian friend, your spouse, or members of your housegroup, compose a litany of praise that covers the key moments in your lives.

- Resolve – as you go about your everyday life and work – to notice someone or something that makes you praise God for His goodness.

- Think of the works of art, the music, the buildings, the landscapes, the books, etc that lead you to bless God for His many blessings.

- Read and reflect on the story of Jacob (Gen. 26–32) and consider how amazing it is that God should be the God of *Jacob*. Think of other 'songs of impossibility'.

AUTUMN SONGS

Autumn Songs: Overture

Worth the Wait! (Psalm 40)

'Top of the Charts' (Psalm 118)

God isn't Hungry (Psalm 50)

PSALMS

'... the autumn leaves ...'

It was a memorable occasion: 'Sung Eucharist' on Easter Day in Ely Cathedral. The mixed-voice choir led us in worship through Haydn's spine-tingling *Nelson Mass* accompanied by orchestra, soprano soloist, trumpeters. Exultation was in the air. Add to that the blue swirls of incense drifting upwards like ascending prayers into the April sunshine streaming down through the great lantern for which Ely is noted. It was an unforgettable multi-sensory experience. I owe my late discovery of the rich tradition of church choral music to that event. 'Eucharist' we call it, from the Greek word *eucharisteo*, 'to give thanks', echoing the moment when Jesus took the cup and gave thanks ...

Songs of thanksgiving are among our favourite psalms. The songs in this category broadly come under what Claus Westermann called 'songs of declarative praise', which give public acknowledgement of God's saving work on our behalf. These songs, as Westermann notes, are particularly products not of the sanctuary but of life 'out there', in the midst of history, yes, while still on the battlefield – in the hour and the place where God acted.[55]

The 'autumn songs' as I have styled them usually tell a story of deliverance and redemption. They are songs of celebration after the crisis is past. Psalms 30, 40, 107, 116, 118 are among these psalms.

Again there is a fairly typical structure to these types of psalms which attentive readers can look out for. Let us take Psalm 116 as an uncomplicated example:

- a declaration of love and praise: 'I love the LORD ...' (v.1)
- a summary of the reason: 'he heard my cry for mercy. Because he turned his ear to me, I will call on him as long as I live' (vv.1–2)
- recall of the particular crisis, in this case a near-death experience: 'The cords of death entangled me ...' (v.3)

- recall of the original petition: 'Then I called on the name of the LORD: "O LORD, save me!"' (v.4)
- expression of praise: 'The LORD is gracious ...' (vv.5–11)
- renewal of vow of praise: 'How can I repay the LORD for all his goodness to me? I will lift up the cup of salvation and call on the name of the LORD ... I will fulfil my vows ...' (vv.12–19).

Walter Brueggemann has characterised these journeys of faith and experience as starting in a state of orientation, collapsing under pressure into disorientation and retrieved by salvation into reorientation.[56]

Orientation describes those satisfied seasons of wellbeing when things are going reasonably smoothly. The songs here celebrate joy, and delight in the continuity and reliability of God's created order.

Disorientation corresponds to seasons of anguished hurt, suffering, pain, injustice, mockery, loneliness, guilt, anger, even rage. Songs at this time channel the pain and resentment to God often in violently emotional language.

Reorientation depicts a state of euphoria at being saved. In these songs, the redeemed are overjoyed at new gifts from God and revel in the turnaround in their fortunes.

Thanksgiving songs vividly capture this last state of 'reorientation'. They express this sense of relief at being rescued, by joyfully charting this saving move from plight to recovery. In them the psalmists are surprised by joy. They are overwhelmed by grace. They rejoice in the new moves and new manifestations of God that have dispelled their despair and dramatically met their needs.

Turning point

The turning point in the psalmist's predicament is often a new resolve of faith, a new and daring act of trust. This is often marked in the text by a 'but I …'. Psalm 31:14 is a case in point. When the simple Hebrew conjunction 'waw' and the first-person singular pronoun start the sentence in this way, emphasis is being placed on the psalmist's change of mood and situation. In Wilson's words, 'It is if he says, "Contrary to what one might expect under the circumstances, I do not despair, but I surrender in trust to the hand of God…" '.[57]

Look for similar turning-points in, for example, Psalms 5:7; 41:4; 52:8; 55:16; 59:16; 69:13; 71:14.

In some psalms the drama of crying to God, being heard and answered is encapsulated in the song by what appears to be an oracle from God given by a priest or prophet. In this way God's answer is interjected, it seems, into the middle of the prayer. We can see this in the abrupt change of voice or tone in Psalms 12:5; 32:8; 50:7; 81:6; 91:14 and so on.

The roots of thanksgiving in Israel lie in the foundational events of the Exodus. Abraham's enslaved descendants cried to the Lord and He heard their cry and delivered them. On this all subsequent thanksgiving songs are patterned. The book of Exodus preserves for us the original response to the miracle of Exodus in the great song of Moses (Exod. 15). Israel was a nation that lived by grace and therefore lived in gratitude: 'Let the redeemed of the LORD say so'. Praise for her was response to covenant mercy and love shown in Yahweh's concrete acts of deliverance and rescue! Praise was born of redemption before it reflected nature.

Israel for this reason never misunderstood praise and thanksgiving as if they were a means of repaying God on an instalment plan! Gratitude is popularly employed in this way. 'He has done all this for you: you must do all for him!' But John Piper has rightly warned against this.[58] As a means of motivating believers to good works it is misplaced. Even the psalmists' commitment to 'paying vows to the Lord', vows made in a time of crisis, should not mislead us into thinking we can repay the debt we owe. To make a vow is to draw further on grace.

Psalm 116 puts the record straight: 'How can I repay the LORD for all his goodness to me? I will lift up the cup of salvation and call on the name of the LORD' (vv.12–13). It is by 'taking' that we pay our vows, by 'calling' on the Lord for help that we honour Him (see Psa. 50). In Piper's memorable words, 'God will not surrender the glory of giving to anyone else.'[59]

In the words of hymnwriter, Robert Robinson:

Come thou fount of every blessing;
Tune my heart to sing thy praise ...
O to grace how great a debtor,
Daily I'm constrained to be.

Grace is a debt we can never repay. We will always be in a negative-equity situation here, thank God!

Thank you!

According to some scholars, it is an oddity of Hebrew that there was no word available by which Old Testament believers could say 'thank you'.[60] Rather, as Westermann puts it, 'Thanking is included entirely within praise.' You thanked someone by telling other people how good or kind that person had been! In other words the way to say 'thank you' was by praising that person in front of others, literally by singing their praises!

Praise of God was therefore by its nature a public declaration by which God was applauded and acclaimed for His mercy and love. It was in this public way that the line between worship and witness was not nearly so sharply drawn as we might suppose. Praising God's greatness and grace in the congregation easily spilled over into public testimony to Him before the listening world and watching nations, who were then summoned and invited to join the chorus of praise raised by the family of faith (so Psa. 96:1,7,10; Psa. 117).

Israel was apparently almost unique in so publicly airing her national identity in this way. In Harvey Guthrie's view, 'Israel is the only people in the Ancient Near East to produce "we" laments and thanksgivings.'[61]

Perhaps too many of our modern praise songs are born of passing moods generated in highly-charged meetings rather than inspired by the deep emotions felt by hearts gripped by redemptive events. Israel's thanksgiving was not born of passing moods or emotional highs or states of spiritual euphoria alone. It was not a case of 'I love You Lord because I feel good about myself today', which is on the road to mushy sentimentality. Israel's thanksgiving was praise for a salvation rooted in remembrance of historic events. It was this that gave rise to Israel's sense of common history celebrated and remembered in such Psalms as 105 and 136 that are liturgical recitals of the great saving events of Israel's history.

Sir Herbert Butterfield, the great Cambridge historian, who wrote also as a Christian said:

> I know of no other case in history where gratitude was carried so far, no other case where gratitude proved to be such a generative thing ... It gave the children of Israel a historical event that they could not get over, could not help remembering and in the first place it made them historians – historians in a way that no one had been before.[62]

Even when they borrowed and adapted nature or harvest festivals from the surrounding pagan culture, Israelite worship leaders turned them into celebrations of historical deliverances, as with Passover, the Feast of Tabernacles. We owe our Bible to their deep sense of thanksgiving. Old Testament history took shape in the

Babylonian exile as the exiles sought desperately to remember and celebrate who they were.

In exile, with Temple and monarchy gone, it was as clear as it had ever been that Israel, now in the midst of a pagan culture, existed – if she existed at all – for the worship and praise of Yahweh, the one true, personal Creator God. Genesis 1 resounded in the exiles' hearts, not as some creation scientist's textbook of proof, but as a great polemical hymn of praise against all idols and in honour of the One Creator God. As W.H. Auden writes:

> Follow poet, follow right
> To the bottom of the night
> With your unconstraining voice
> Still persuade us to rejoice
>
> In the deserts of the heart
> Let the healing fountain start
> In the prison of his days
> Teach the free man how to praise[63]

Thanksgiving in Israel was not only public praise but sacrificial offering (see Lev. 7:12ff). This is reflected in the Psalms (see Psa. 107:8, 21–22, 32; and especially Psa. 50).

A direct line, although one which passes through the crucial transformer of the cross, connects such practices and psalms with the saving events celebrated in the Christian gospel (Heb. 13:12–15).

New covenant worshippers acknowledge gladly that the ultimate thank-offering – as it was the final sin offering – was the offering of the Lord Jesus Christ to His Father on the altar of the cross. Not surprisingly, it is the Greek word for 'giving thanks' that has adhered to our commemoration of His sacrifice, 'the Eucharist'.

Worth the Wait! (Psalm 40)

For the director of music. Of David. A psalm.

¹I waited patiently for the LORD;
    he turned to me and heard my cry.
²He lifted me out of the slimy pit,
    out of the mud and mire;
he set my feet on a rock
    and gave me a firm place to stand.
³He put a new song in my mouth,
    a hymn of praise to our God.
Many will see and fear
    and put their trust in the LORD.

⁴Blessed is the man
    who makes the LORD his trust,
who does not look to the proud,
    to those who turn aside to false gods.
⁵Many, O LORD my God,
    are the wonders you have done.
The things you planned for us
    no-one can recount to you;
were I to speak and tell of them,
    they would be too many to declare.

⁶Sacrifice and offering you did not desire,
    but my ears you have pierced;
burnt offerings and sin offerings
    you did not require.
⁷Then I said, 'Here I am, I have come –
    it is written about me in the scroll.
⁸I desire to do your will, O my God;
    your law is within my heart.'

[9]I proclaim righteousness in the great assembly;
    I do not seal my lips,
    as you know, O LORD.
[10]I do not hide your righteousness in my heart;
    I speak of your faithfulness and salvation.
I do not conceal your love and your truth
    from the great assembly.

[11]Do not withhold your mercy from me, O LORD;
    may your love and your truth always protect me.
[12]For troubles without number surround me;
    my sins have overtaken me, and I cannot see.
They are more than the hairs of my head,
    and my heart fails within me.

[13]Be pleased, O LORD, to save me;
    O LORD, come quickly to help me.
[14]May all who seek to take my life
    be put to shame and confusion;
may all who desire my ruin
    be turned back in disgrace.
[15]May those who say to me, 'Aha! Aha!'
    be appalled at their own shame.
[16]But may all who seek you
    rejoice and be glad in you;
may those who love your salvation always say,
    'The LORD be exalted!'

[17]Yet I am poor and needy;
    may the Lord think of me.
You are my help and my deliverer;
    O my God, do not delay.

IT WAS ONE OF TV'S MOST POPULAR SHOWS. EMERGENCY services are put on full alert; blue lights flash; engines snarl and tyres squeal as they speed into action. Firefighters and paramedics rush to the scene. Ropes, axes, cranes, heavy-lifting gear, even helicopters are put to work. The place swarms with hard-hatted, yellow-coated rescue workers under blazing arc lights. The desperate victim is either trapped under teetering masonry, or is up to his neck in quicksand, or unconscious on a narrow ledge halfway up or down the frozen mountain. The show was called '999' – a vivid and authentic reconstruction of real-life dramas.

Psalm 40 is a reconstruction of a real-life drama, the life-saving act of rescue and the life-changing consequences of being saved!

The psalmist has something to sing about (vv.1–3)!

His sense of relief is overwhelming. All the more so for being a near-run thing. What took you so long? I thought you were never coming!

'I waited patiently ...' the psalmist recalls

Waiting is the hardest bit of all isn't it? The tension before guests arrive is one thing, sitting in the dentist's waiting-room another, waiting to go on stage is altogether different again. But these are as nothing compared to being stuck in quicksand with your body slowly slipping beneath the slimy mud, hope rapidly drowning and desperation surely rising. Your whole life, if not exactly flashing before you, then at least slowly drags itself through your consciousness.

How long? How long? Had the psalmist really 'waited patiently' we wonder?

'Come off it,' we're tempted to reply. 'Surely you are exercising some poetic licence here? Isn't hindsight perhaps embroidering the testimony just a little?' Whatever the reality of the psalmist's patience, there is no doubt about the genuineness of his sense of relief. And that huge sigh of relief is something only the rescued know.

The psalmist has found something to sing about!

So here is this ancient troubadour of Israel, 'safe and sound and singing' and celebrating God's rescue. In his immense joy, he is clear about what he wants us to know.

God gave me a hearing: 'he turned to me and heard my cry' (v.1b)

Thanks be to God that He is a listening God. This has been Israel's experience from the beginning. In fact this is how it all began. Slaves in Egypt, they cried out to the Lord and He heard them and acted to save them (Exod. 2:23–25). The cry for help was Israel's primal scream; redemption is God's primary reply.

God gave a new start: 'He lifted me out of the slimy pit ...' (v.2)

My predicament was deep and dark and damning. But He reached down and rescued me. Once I was 'down and out'; now I am 'up and in'. Once I was blind but now I see.

To get out of the black holes that sin digs for us is often messy and sometimes rough. But getting out covers a multitude of scars. Getting out is what matters most. Cleaning-up can follow. Now is the time for jubilant shouts and hearty backslapping and vigorous hugging and joy-filled dancing. Pose for the pictures right there and then. Never forget the moment you were saved. Always remember why the champagne flowed.

God gave me a new security: 'he set my feet on a rock and gave me a firm place to stand' (v.2b)

I find a firm footing in God's truth and love instead of the swamp of self-delusion. I feel like Archimedes now. Give me a place to stand and I can move the world!

God gave me a new song: 'He put a new song in my mouth, a hymn of praise to our God' (v.3)

These are the new songs we need. Not the latest compositions to roll off the charismatic assembly line, welcome as they often are. But the singing of every song, ancient and modern, with the freshness and fierce joy of those who have never forgotten the relief at being rescued.

I endorse P.T. Forsyth's plea as a word for our time: 'We want the breathless awe, and the stammering tongue, and the solemn wonder, and the passionate gratitude – which are the true note of grace, and the worship of a soul plucked from the burning and snatched by a miracle from the abyss. We want the new song of those who stand upon the rock, taken from the fearful pit and the miry clay with the trembling still upon them and the slime still moist.[64]

Is your slime, as it were, still moist?
Do I tremble at all?
Do we still smell singed?
Are we breathless, stammering, solemn, passionate in praise?
The forgiven love much
the recently forgiven more so,
the drastically forgiven most of all.

You may be surprised by your audience: 'Many will see and fear and put their trust in the LORD' (v.3b).

There is a world out there that is watching for the alchemy that transforms lives. There are those who are tired of celebration without victory, weary of entertainment without joy who are longing for something worth making a song and dance about. These satiated and over-stimulated ones are waiting for their breath to be taken away, slain by the enchantment of a deeper magic. They secretly yearn to be frightened out of their fears, and they are growing sick and tired of self-dependency and addiction to self-trust. That fierce opponent of our faith, the German philosopher, Frederick Nietzsche, rightly challenged us when he said that only if Christians looked more redeemed, would he ever consider conversion. So the praise of the truly redeemed affirms faith in God and repudiates all idolatry. Praise discounts all false gods (v.4b).

This is not the sort of touchy-feely, 'God-is-my-girlfriend' session that passes for praise in some parts of the contemporary Church. True Praise is an abandonment of trust to the mighty and majestic one. As for the psalmist, he wishes he had 'ten thousand tongues' to 'sing his great Redeemer's praise' (v.5). Ours is an incomparable God. Ten thousand tongues would not be enough to recount all God's loving thoughts, and mighty deeds on our behalf! If I had all eternity it would be too short to sing my Saviour's praise.

At this point exuberant praise softens into reflection (vv.6–8).

Our best theology is doxology. Our best thinking about God is done as we rise from our knees or when the music stops as we rest from our rejoicing.

God gave me a new script (vv.6–8)

At the height of the musical drama, the psalmist pauses to wonder that he has been picked for the cast, that his destiny is 'written in the scroll'.

In pausing to reflect, the psalmist realises that 'sacrifice and offering' are not in the end what God wants. But didn't God Himself legislate for animal sacrifices and offerings in the Law? Yes, but what God desires is deeper than what He demands, what He requires more fundamental than what He prescribes. God really wants obedience from the 'heart' (v.8). This is symbolised by 'ears' that are 'pierced' and made attentive to His summons (v.6b), perhaps echoing Exodus 21:6, where a slave is claimed for his master by having his ear pierced by an awl to the doorpost. Alternatively, the image may suggest ears that are 'dug' so that, as a well is unblocked, so our ears are unplugged to listen to God.

Either way the point is clear. The psalmist comes to see that what God is after is the heart which loves and obeys and which alone makes sacrificial worship meaningful.

It dawns on him afresh that the life-saving experience of rescue has become a life-changing vocation of salvation. Full of song, he finds his ears open to the melodies of heaven, to the tunes of glory, to the music of eternity. Once tone-deaf through sin, his ears are now opened to the master composer and His masterly music. He is captivated by what he hears! 'Then I said: "Here I am, I have come – it is written about me in the scroll"' (v.7). Our singer rejoices to find himself written into the script of God's musical drama! Some scholars suggest that this phrase – 'written in the scroll' – reflects the practice of presenting a written narrative of one's testimony to the Lord at the Temple. Whatever the truth of that suggestion, it is clear that the psalmist rejoices that he has been chosen for a part.

He resolves to play that part to the full … 'I desire to do your will, O my God; your law is within my heart' (v.8).

This is the joy of being personally involved, with our own part to play. This is the joy of those who have found the script of what the truly human life is all about. The praising heart which has discovered this, delights to be in God's drama, wants to sing in tune with God, wants to see what God sees, think what God thinks and love what God loves.

These verses are quoted in the New Testament by the writer to the Hebrews and applied to the Lord Jesus (Heb. 10:5–7). Placed in the heart and mouth of the Lord Jesus as He comes into the world in incarnation, they reveal the deep obedience and love for His Father that Jesus carried in His heart. He was the greatest embodiment of these words. But we may note that the psalmist's sequence is reversed when applied to Jesus!

In the psalmist's train of thought, what lies beyond sacrifice is obedience and this leads to the profound spirituality of being one heart and mind and will with God. But Jesus makes the move in the other direction. He started out totally at one with the Father's heart and mind and will: 'I delight to do your will.' Then He embraced the servant's role of availability and obedience: 'Here I am, I have come to do your will, as it is written about me in the scroll.' Finally, in union with His Father and in the spirit of obedient servanthood, He chose to become obedient to death and give Himself in sacrifice on the cross.

The law in His heart was second nature to Him. The writer to the Hebrews significantly cuts short the quotation at this point. Jesus was only doing what came naturally. We can love like this only by doing what comes supernaturally. It is His song we learn to sing in our celebration of salvation and His second advent we prepare for in our weekly rehearsals every Sunday.

Now our singer is ready to go public (vv.9–10)

He's ready to join the hallelujah chorus!

'I do not conceal your love and your truth from the great assembly.'

Praise is personal: 'I proclaim ... I do not seal my lips ...'

Praise is vocal: we are not frozen at the mouth like Canadian rivers in winter!

And then praise is public: join the chorus, tell all, be bold.

How much does your rescue mean to you? I do not ask: 'Do the songs turn you on, emotionally'? How much does your rescue and your Redeemer stir you?

As John Piper says, 'You can't commend what you don't cherish.'

As that eccentric, early Cornish Methodist, Billy Bray boasted: 'Lock me in a barrel and I'd praise the Lord through the bunghole'!

Suddenly (vv.11–17), the psalm takes a strange turn. From rejoicing over being rescued, the psalmist pleads for help from fresh trouble! Desperate praying ensues. There are new attacks from unexpected quarters, from enemies old or new. Troubles intensify. Besetting sins almost obliterate his vision of the future. Hope falters. Contrary to the false reports of the over-sanguine, being saved, it seems, does not make you immune from further distress.

So the psalmist pleads for help again. But it is not a self-serving prayer. It is all thoroughly God-centred.

God saved us and we are grateful.

God alone is worthy of trust.

God's wonders and thoughts are overwhelming.

God claims our allegiance, ears and mind and heart
   and will.

God is the theme of our singing and celebration.

Therefore, the psalmist assures us, we can be confident that God will again provide and save.

Those who love God's salvation have no difficulty giving credit where all credit is due: 'The LORD be exalted!' (v.16).

The only hope we have that God is *love* is that God is *God*!

The Lord is exalted even while 'I am poor and needy' (v.17).

This is exactly what makes salvation work and thanksgiving called for.

'Not what I am but what thou art, That, that alone can be my soul's true rest'.[65]

'May those who love your salvation always say, "The LORD be exalted!"'.

So, paradoxically, but true to life, a song which began with testimony that the psalmist had 'waited patiently' (v.1) now ends with a rather impatient psalmist urging: 'hurry up God – I can't wait for ever!' (v.17b). After all, if God is worth praising fervently, and listening to obediently, then God is well worth waiting for.

'Top of the Charts' (Psalm 118)

[1]Give thanks to the LORD, for he is good;
   his love endures for ever.

[2]Let Israel say:
   'His love endures for ever.'
[3]Let the house of Aaron say:
   'His love endures for ever.'
[4]Let those who fear the LORD say:
   'His love endures for ever.'

[5]In my anguish I cried to the LORD,
   and he answered by setting me free.
[6]The LORD is with me; I will not be afraid.
   What can man do to me?
[7]The LORD is with me; he is my helper.
   I will look in triumph on my enemies.

[8]It is better to take refuge in the LORD
   than to trust in man.
[9]It is better to take refuge in the LORD
   than to trust in princes.

[10]All the nations surrounded me,
   but in the name of the LORD I cut them off.
[11]They surrounded me on every side,
   but in the name of the LORD I cut them off.
[12]They swarmed around me like bees,
   but they died out as quickly as burning thorns;
   in the name of the LORD I cut them off.

[13]I was pushed back and about to fall,
   but the LORD helped me.

¹⁴The Lord is my strength and my song;
    he has become my salvation.

¹⁵Shouts of joy and victory
    resound in the tents of the righteous:
'The Lord's right hand has done mighty things!
¹⁶   The Lord's right hand is lifted high;
    the Lord's right hand has done mighty things!'

¹⁷I will not die but live,
    and will proclaim what the Lord has done.
¹⁸The Lord has chastened me severely,
    but he has not given me over to death.
¹⁹Open for me the gates of righteousness;
    I will enter and give thanks to the Lord.
²⁰This is the gate of the Lord
    through which the righteous may enter.
²¹I will give you thanks, for you answered me;
    you have become my salvation.

²²The stone the builders rejected
    has become the capstone;
²³the Lord has done this,
    and it is marvellous in our eyes.
²⁴This is the day the Lord has made;
    let us rejoice and be glad in it.

²⁵O Lord, save us;
    O Lord, grant us success.
²⁶Blessed is he who comes in the name of the Lord.
    From the house of the Lord we bless you.
²⁷The Lord is God,
    and he has made his light shine upon us.
With boughs in hand, join in the festal procession

up to the horns of the altar.

[28]You are my God, and I will give thanks;
you are my God, and I will exalt you.

[29]Give thanks to the LORD, for he is good;
his love endures for ever.

I BELONG TO THE GENERATION OLD ENOUGH TO REMEMBER chart-topping popular songs that actually stuck in your mind so that you could hum them in the street or sing them, even if only in the bath. Buddy Holly, Elvis, even the Beatles. Their lyrics may have been banal but the tunes were catchy and arose unbidden from the back of your memory any time. How true is this, I wonder, nowadays?

You never forget a good tune. But here's an odd thing. What happened to the music of the psalms, no one knows. No doubt the melody and instrumental accompaniment and vocal settings of the psalms varied over the centuries. But God, for His own good reasons, providentially chose not to preserve them. Some years ago, a French musicologist, Suzanne Haik Vantoura, claimed to have rediscovered ancient biblical music. (You can judge for yourself whether her efforts are convincing by listening to the CD, *The Music of the Bible*; a thousand-year-old notation deciphered, Harmonia Mundi, 195989, 1976/2000).

But the lyrics survived. One in particular remained 'Top of the Pops' in Israel for 500 years! Kings came and went, empires waxed and waned, but throughout Israel's turbulent history, one lyric stayed the course. It was a crisp, unforgettable two-line celebration of God's covenant-love:

Give thanks to the LORD for he is good;
his [covenant-love] endures for ever.

Whether in simple folk-song setting for the hillside, or in sophisticated choral anthem arrangement for the Temple, this was the one song all Israel loved to sing.

Liturgists have tried to unravel the ritual involved in the psalm. It's intriguing to speculate with them.

The psalm suggests a dramatic and impressive ceremony. We hear the priest perhaps making the call to worship and inviting response (vv.1–4). A solo voice gives thanks that the Lord stood by him when in need (vv.5–6). A reflective comment is then sung, perhaps by the choir (vv.8–9). Was it the king who once sang these lines as the nation's representative? 'All the nations surrounded me …' (vv.10–12). Was it the royal voice we hear that first declares, 'The LORD is my strength and my song; he has become my salvation' (vv.13–14)? Next comes a victory song, maybe taken up by the choir (vv.15–16). And again a single voice; perhaps the king, renews his determination to proclaim publicly what the Lord has done for him and his people (vv.17–19).

Then the king and his party approach the door of the sanctuary and request that it be opened to let them in (v.19)! To which the gatekeepers, perhaps, reply: 'This is the gate of the LORD through which the righteous may enter' (v.20).

The king again states his resolve to give God thanks (v.21).

The priest replies in memorable and prophetic language that the time has come for God's achievements to be acclaimed (vv.22–24).

The Temple singers continue to offer prayers and invitations, as the festal procession, with shouted hosannas, wends its way into the sanctuary (vv.25–27). The individual worshipper makes a final acclamation (v.28). The finale is a full-throated, whole-hearted choral appeal to 'give thanks to the LORD, for he is good, for his [covenant-love] endures for ever' (v.29).

This is the heart and soul of Israel's eucharist: the covenant-love of the LORD. 'Covenant-love' or 'hesed' is variously translated as steadfast love, mercy, unfailing love, loyal love. It is here that the faith of the believing community is most fully articulated. Here is expressed its most fundamental conviction about God.

God is love. Love which is no fleeting emotion or passing mood. This is love which makes covenant commitments and keeps them whatever the cost. This is love that puts itself under a self-imposed obligation to save whatever the price that has to be paid. This is tough love. Here is a love which turns up however bad the call. Here is the love of the covenant LORD that stays true in any circumstances. You can sing of it any time.

(1) *You can sing this song on a day of dedication* (vv.1–4).

Israel did.

It's not hard to imagine the dramatic ritual of the occasion. As the liturgy unfolds, the procession makes its way with antiphonal responses, priests inquire and people answer. Each tribal representative is called upon to affirm this confidence: 'Let the house of Aaron say: "His love endures for ever." '

When David dedicated his tent-sanctuary in Jerusalem this was the theme of the song sung by the prophetic Levitical singers (1 Chron. 16:34).

When Solomon later dedicated the Temple this was the song sung which evoked the glory cloud (2 Chron. 5:13; 7:3).

When the litany of Israel's history is rehearsed in the worshipping assembly, this is the repeated refrain (Psa. 136).

(2) *You can sing this song on a day of deliverance* (vv. 5–9).

Many in Israel did.

'In my anguish I cried to the LORD, and he answered me by setting me free' (v.5). What the singer here, perhaps the king, could bear witness to, others could endorse from their own life-stories. Psalm 107 offers ample evidence. And as the old saying goes, those with an experience are never at the mercy of those with an argument! The personal testimonies line up to take the stand.

Wanderers (Psa. 107:4–9) in a wilderness of their own choosing, the mark of Cain upon them, have lost their way. Emaciated and weak from hunger and thirst, they eventually cry to the Lord: and He delivers them from their distress. The desperate get saved where the self-satisfied do not. 'Let them give thanks to the LORD for his unfailing love'.

Prisoners (Psa. 107:10–16) incarcerated in their self-imposed captivity, rebels, as we all are, in defiance of God's Word, caught with the weapons of insurrection in their hands, the sons of disobedience, find that self-fulfilment is a dead-end street: they cry to the Lord and He saves them and sets them free. 'Let them give thanks to the LORD for his unfailing love'.

Sufferers (Psa. 107:17–22) in a satiated society who have had too much of a good thing, whose lust for promiscuous living has made them sick, whose addictions have well nigh killed them, cry to the Lord and He hears and heals them. 'Let them give thanks to the LORD for his unfailing love'.

Voyagers (Psa. 107:23–32) who thought they knew better than anyone how to negotiate the ocean of life, find themselves terrifyingly swamped by huge breakers. Sharp people who have lived by their wits now find themselves at their wits' end. Those who trusted in their own expertise and navigational life skills, cry out for help from sinking ships like any other drowning man! But the Lord hears and saves them in their distress and rights their craft and brings them to the desired harbour.

Whether in desert straits, dark dungeons, at death's door, or simply out of your depth, 'whoever is wise' would do well to 'heed these things and consider the great love of the LORD' (Psa. 107:43). Reflecting on these vivid testimonies, let the redeemed say: 'God is good, his covenant-love endures for ever.'

Only covenant-love is enduring love, not just an emergency service.

In every case, this love proves to be homeward bound as well as outward bound. It comes to where we are to rescue us, but takes us back to home and harbour, there to be redeemed, restored to health and made whole.

Refocusing on Psalm 118 we see that ...

(3) *You can sing this song of covenant-love on a day of victory* (vv. 10–18).

Israel did.

Folk memories still lingered of how the nation had begun its life in Exodus (15:13). Now it is a time of national crisis. The king is alarmed: 'All the nations surrounded me.' The enemies in coalition swarm round God's people like hostile bees. The king, Jehoshaphat, feels personally threatened. Royal and public intercession is made: 'We do not know what to do but our eyes are upon you' (2 Chron. 20:12).

Step forward a Spirit-anointed prophet. 'Do not be afraid or discouraged ... the battle is not yours, but God's ... Go out to face them tomorrow, and the LORD will be with you' (2 Chron. 20:15,17). Unusually, in the Old Testament history, the king heeds the prophet. King and people bow in worshipful acceptance of the Lord's reassuring word. 'Have faith in God's prophets', advises the king, 'and you will be successful'(2 Chron. 20:20). In an unprecedented and risky act of faith, Jehoshaphat sets a choir at the head of the army. Notice what they sing. Not marching songs meant simply to raise morale among the fighters. Not stirring and aggressive war songs directed at the enemy. But a song that celebrates God's covenant-love! Nothing routs the enemies of God and His people more than being confronted by believers in the full armour of praise. It is not the love of power but the power of love that prevails.

Read the Chronicler's account again (2 Chron. 20). You can almost hear the king penning the words of Psalm 118:14, 'The LORD is my strength and my song'. Any war correspondent would surely have reported, 'Shouts of joy and victory resound in the tents of the righteous ... "The LORD's right hand has done mighty things" ' (vv.15–16).

(4) *You can sing this song on a day of restoration* (vv.19–24). And Israel did.

Even after being swallowed up by the rapacious expansionist policy of the Babylonian Empire, Israel learns to sing this song again. For the sake of His covenant-love, God moves in mysterious ways His wonders to perform, not least in the way He raises up the Persian leader Cyrus, as His unwitting instrument of liberation for His exiled people. When Cyrus conquers the Babylonians, he reverses the social engineering policies of Babylon, and opts to send the deported people back to their own homelands.

So amid the shattered landscape of Jerusalem and the broken ruins of the Temple, a rough stone altar is erected. It's a small but significant start in rebuilding a nation for God. Waste no time: let's celebrate. Old harps, once hung in despair on the nearest willow tree, are dusted off and restrung.

Half-remembered songs, embarrassingly under-used in strange lands, soon spring to mind again. One song in particular – as the far-sighted Jeremiah had foretold – says what everyone is feeling. Ezra masterminds the celebration. Priests resplendent in vestments blow trumpets, and the sons of Asaph with cymbals lead the praise and thanksgiving as they sing to the Lord: 'He is good; his love to Israel endures for ever' (Ezra 3:10–11; see Jer. 33:11 for the prophet's earlier assurance).

What an occasion!

The LORD's – door is open – enter through it.
The LORD's – deed is done – marvel at it.
The LORD's – day is here – rejoice in it.

But here we modern worshippers have the advantage over ancient kings, prophets, and psalmists. 'Blessed are the eyes that see what you see. For I tell you that many prophets and kings wanted to see what you see but did not see it, and to hear what you hear but did not hear it' (Luke 10:23–24).

One day, centuries after the Psalms' origin, a festive procession wound its way up to the Temple Mount. Given the over-flowing nature of this self-giving love, it has always seemed likely that the carefully-crafted liturgical 'hosannas' – 'O LORD save us' (Psa. 118:25) – would, one day 'spill over onto the streets unrehearsed and unliturgical ...'.[66]

(5) *For this is the day of Redemption (vv.25–29)*
The door of God's kingdom is being flung open not for the righteous but for sinners who repent and are 'righteoused' by faith!

'The LORD has done this, and it is marvellous in our eyes' (v.23).

This is the day of salvation and many rejoice in it as they watch the lonely figure, dispensing healing on the way, striding towards the cross to prove God's covenant-love even to His enemies.

And then, to cap it all, comes the day of resurrection!

Now truly the gate of deathless glory is opened, a great hole is blasted in death's wall and the door into God's resurrection realm is flung wide.

This is the Lord's doing and assuredly no one else's!

He takes the One rejected by the expert temple-builders as not fitting in with their plans for God's house and elevates Him to be the highest headstone of it all.

Today is truly the Lord's day – the day of resurrection, the first day of the first week of new creation.

Martin Luther said: 'This is a psalm which I love – for truly it has deserved well of me many a time and has delivered me from many a sore affliction when neither emperor nor kings nor the wise nor the cunning nor the saints were able or willing to help me.'

Let's sing of the covenant-love of the Lord that will not let us go or let us down.

This song never goes out of fashion.

This is truly a song for all seasons.

God isn't Hungry (Psalm 50)

A psalm of Asaph.

[1]The Mighty One, God, the LORD,
　　speaks and summons the earth
　　from the rising of the sun to the place where it sets.
[2]From Zion, perfect in beauty,
　　God shines forth.
[3]Our God comes and will not be silent;
　　a fire devours before him,
　　and around him a tempest rages.
[4]He summons the heavens above,
　　and the earth, that he may judge his people:
[5]'Gather to me my consecrated ones,
　　who made a covenant with me by sacrifice.'
[6]And the heavens proclaim his righteousness,
　　for God himself is judge.　　　　　　　　*Selah*

[7]'Hear, O my people, and I will speak,
　　O Israel, and I will testify against you:
　　I am God, your God.
[8]I do not rebuke you for your sacrifices
　　or your burnt offerings, which are ever before me.
[9]I have no need of a bull from your stall
　　or of goats from your pens,
[10]for every animal of the forest is mine,
　　and the cattle on a thousand hills.
[11]I know every bird in the mountains,
　　and the creatures of the field are mine.
[12]If I were hungry I would not tell you,
　　for the world is mine, and all that is in it.
[13]Do I eat the flesh of bulls
　　or drink the blood of goats?

¹⁴Sacrifice thank-offerings to God,
    fulfil your vows to the Most High,
¹⁵and call upon me in the day of trouble;
    I will deliver you, and you will honour me.'

¹⁶But to the wicked, God says:

'What right have you to recite my laws
    or take my covenant on your lips?
¹⁷You hate my instruction
    and cast my words behind you.
¹⁸When you see a thief, you join with him;
    you throw in your lot with adulterers.
¹⁹You use your mouth for evil
    and harness your tongue to deceit.
²⁰You speak continually against your brother
    and slander your own mother's son.
²¹These things you have done and I kept silent;
    you thought I was altogether like you.
But I will rebuke you
    and accuse you to your face.

²²'Consider this, you who forget God,
    or I will tear you to pieces, with none to rescue:
²³He who sacrifices thank-offerings honours me,
    and he prepares the way
    so that I may show him the salvation of God.'

A FANFARE ANNOUNCES THE ENTRANCE OF THE JUDGE.
The court is in session. The whole earth is summoned to attend.
The roll call of names is impressive:

- v.1: 'El' – the chief God,
- v.14: 'El Elyon' – the Most High God,

- v.1: 'Elohim' – God, the Creator and life-giver. Most important of all:
- v.1: 'Yahweh' – LORD of grace and covenant is named.

And the Lord answers to them all as He arrives to convene the meeting of the court. He speaks and the whole world attends; He shines forth like the dawn rising on the earth; He sweeps on to the scene and the shockwaves reverberate around the natural world. Thunder rolls, lightning flashes, storm winds swirl around Him. Here is the One Creator God on the move. This is the classic language of theophany reminiscent of the momentous meeting on Sinai at the start of Israel's national story (Exod. 19).

But His consuming interest is His people, Israel. He has come to summon them to a covenant renewal: 'gather to me my consecrated ones, who made a covenant with me by sacrifice' (v.5). God arrives as Judge. He comes to settle a covenant lawsuit with Israel. He is here to evaluate the relationship between Him and His people. The natural phenomena that attend Him are a sign of the importance of this relationship for all creation. Heaven and earth are involved not simply to add stunning audio-visual effects but to act as legal witnesses to this lawsuit with His people. Moses, similarly, has invoked creation to testify to the weight of his words to Israel (Deut. 32:1).

The witnesses confirm that God has proved righteous in making and keeping covenant with Israel (v.6). His faithfulness is beyond dispute; but what of the fidelity of the 'faithful ones' consecrated to covenant partnership with Him (v.5)? This marks a permanent pause for thought on the part of God's people. Before we rail at the wider world or bemoan the pagan society around us, we must remind ourselves that judgment begins with the household of God (1 Pet. 4:17).

The majestic opening alerts us to the main complaint God has against His people – that of underestimating Him. As we have noted, the fire and storm imagery recall the making of the covenant with Israel at the majestic mountain of Sinai. Now it is from Jerusalem's humble hill of Zion that He shines forth and speaks.

This movement *from Sinai to Zion* is very significant. It represents a further revelation of His grace and presence. But it is a movement we can also dangerously misunderstand. At Sinai God dwelt in unapproachable majesty; at Zion God invites men to dwell with Him. At Sinai God's transcendence repels us; at Zion His immanence attracts us. At Sinai He keeps His distance from us; at Zion He draws near to us. The movement from the towering heights of holiness at Sinai to the humbler hill of Zion is a movement downwards, a condescension of God from mystery to intimacy, from being wholly 'above' us to being 'with us' (cf. Psa. 46; 48).

But it is just here that we can seriously misread him. We make a big error if we mistake His condescension for a reduction in His majesty. If we dissolve the vital tension between His 'farness' and His nearness then we presume on His intimacy and make Him altogether too cosy, too familiar and too user-friendly a God.

But His 'come down' to Zion is no cut down in size! He retains even in close-up all His majesty and mightiness. He refuses to be underestimated. In the covenant lawsuit enacted in the psalm, He re-asserts his 'Godness' to His people. Secure in covenant relationship with Him we may be, but we dare not domesticate Him, trivialise Him, or reduce His heavyweight glory.

Now the One who is 'God, your God' speaks (v.7).

He reissues the basic summons to 'hear' – the 'shema' of Deuteronomy 6:4 – which gathers an attentive people and distinguishes them as a people of the Word.

In the next two sections of the psalm (vv.7–15 and 16–23), God addresses two aspects of our underestimation of Him, and pinpoints two mistakes we make about Him.

(1) *In verses 7–15 God indicts His people for formalism in worship.*

Speaking through a prophet, He summons His people to evaluate their worship. In particular, He confronts them with the urgent need to reassess the meaning of the sacrifices they make to Him. In the history of biblical interpretation, statements like this have often been taken to imply that God was repudiating all ritual offerings in favour of a more spiritual worship. This is unlikely. God is not, at this point of time, rejecting sacrifices; after all He ordained them (v.8). The point is: He doesn't need them (v.9).

'He owns "The cattle on a thousand hills"' (v. 10), words which I sang as a small child in Sunday School too long ago for polite memory to mention. But they were indelibly inscribed on my childish heart, and every decade since has confirmed their truth. Everything belongs to God in the first place (vv.8–10). The promised land was always 'His Land' of whom Israel was a tenant. The earth is the Lord's of which we are all only stewards. However significant our roles in His service we remain under-shepherds of His flock, under-managers of His estate. Perhaps the import of this has still to shape our debates about the technological use, and abuse, of the environment.

What God wants, it seems, is loving, thankful, obedient hearts in those who worship Him by sacrifice. What He wants is sensitive and responsible handling of His good earth and its resources. What He desires is wise stewardship of the dominion He has delegated to us over His wonderful world.

The picture offered to us next in this prophetic psalm is hilarious. It is the comic image of a hungry God (v.12)! Even if He were to get hungry He wouldn't tell us because He can whistle up roast beef any time He chooses! What He really hungers for are worshippers who give Him thanks, pay their vows, depend on Him for help in prayers offered, and praise Him for prayers answered (vv.14–15) – compare John 4:23. Nothing pleases Him more than being called upon to live up to His name as Saviour of His people. Worshipping Him is not the sacrifice we make but the sacrifice we trust. 'This psalm is one of the most exalted statements we have of God's goodness.' It 'resists the notion that Yahweh is a consumer or client of Israel.'[67]

In short, we cannot supply God. God is no man's debtor. 'Who has ever given to God, that God should repay him?' (Rom. 11:35; see also Isa. 40:13). Sacrifice your thank-offerings but these are only an acknowledgement of His sufficiency. The more we thank, the more we prepare the way for Him to show us more grace. The more we pay our vows the more indebted to grace we become!

'How can I repay the LORD for all his goodness to me? I will lift ... and call ...' (Psa. 116:12ff).

Early in my theological learning I remember being attracted to a statement about the gospel and its response that went something like this: 'Salvation is grace and ethics is gratitude.' And, of course, it encapsulated a valid truth, that all our good works are an outflow of an initiative God has taken. But John Piper has recently – and rightly in my view – questioned this popular nostrum. He seeks to wean us off what he calls 'the debtor's ethic'. Gratitude is at the heart of praise and thanksgiving but as a motive for holy living, Piper warns, it contains hidden dangers. We often hear it said that 'God has done so much for you: what will you do for Him?' Unfortunately, what this is often taken to mean, in practice, is that 'good deeds and religious acts are the installment payments we make on the unending debt we owe God'.

Even the paying of vows should not be misconstrued. In Piper's words, '"paying vows" in the Old Testament is not part of the debtor's ethic. It is an act of faith in future grace. Pay your vows, that is, call on me in the day of trouble, and I will rescue you with future grace. And you will give me honor'.[68]

As Piper says, in a sentence that cries out to be quoted, 'God will not surrender the glory of being the Giver.'[69]

This refutes one common mistake we make as worshippers. It is to assume that our activity somehow makes up some lack in God, covers some deficiency in Him, or plugs some gap in His resources! But, as has been well said: 'even if all the prodigal sons came home on the same day that would not put the Father in an embarrassing position.' Yet how many mission appeals made to the Church imply that God cannot manage on His own, is a bit hard-pressed, has over-stretched His resources, and needs our help if His enterprise is not to fail?

Nor do we always avoid the trap of thinking that our activity somehow puts God in our debt! Again Psalm 50 punctures such illusions by reminding us that He has ample supplies and doesn't need what we can give. This is not the kingdom of man with God to serve in it but the kingdom of God with man to serve in it. We find His monopoly of giving hard to accept. If only I prayed more, fasted myself thinner, praised more vociferously, confessed God's Word more consistently, attended church more often, gave more money … then He would be obliged to bless me! But God is under obligation to no one but Himself. In any case, our God is far less religious than we are. God is more interested in life.

(2) *So in verses 16–23 we find His indictment of His people's hypocrisy.*

Here is exposed that fatal divorce of worship and work, praise and living. Here is a classic 'prophetic' rebuke of worship detached from life – a theme running from Amos, through this psalm, the Sermon on the Mount, to the letter of James. Here are condemned a people going through the motions of paying lip-service to a God whom they speedily 'forget' once they are outside the sanctuary. God 'contemporises the commandments'.[70]

God confronts those who recite the Ten Commandments in worship and break them in the work-place and the bedroom. Adultery, stealing, slander are the transgressions God chooses to highlight (vv.18–20).

And the great failure again is to underestimate God. We assume that because He is patient with us He is conniving at our insincerity and hypocrisy (v.21). We take His silence for acquiescence in our double-lives. And we are wrong. For God is not the invisible backdrop to life whom for all practical purposes we can ignore. He is not the unseen guest at every transaction. Now He shows up!

Nor is He the silent spectator of all our double-dealing. Now He speaks! 'The non-intervention of God bears a very heavy interest and he is greatly to be feared when he does nothing. He moves in long orbits out of sight and sound. But he always arrives.'[71]

The mistake again is to misread God's intimacy. 'You thought I was altogether like you' (v.21). God graciously condescends to present Himself to us in human terms as someone who has a face and hands and eyes, who speaks and hears, decides and feels and acts as we do. But at this very point, where He appears in human guise, we are in most danger of devaluing His deity. It is precisely at this point He reasserts his 'Godness' (compare with Hosea 11:9).

In holiness, in faithfulness, in integrity He is most decidedly not like us. God refuses to be remade in our image. He cannot be presumed upon as God who 'nods and winks' at our inconsistencies, who smiles knowingly at our blatant hypocrisy, who offers repeat prescriptions of forgiveness to order.

When the real God reappears it's more a slap in the face than a pat on the back (v.21b). God is no church mouse but the lion that roars and tears (v.22). Covenant-breakers beware.

And yet when God comes in such splendour and with such penetrating analysis, it is not to obviate our worship but to cleanse and renew it. A new way of worship is opened up to us. To thank Him in the abandoned surrender of gratitude is to honour Him as He wants to be honoured and to open the way for further displays of His amazing grace. Who would want to underestimate Him whose final word is 'salvation' (v.23)?

Certainly not Christians in worship.

We know our great Redeemer came not to be sacrificed to but to sacrifice and to give His life a ransom for many. Our first – and last – duty of service is to be ministered to by His sacrifice for us. By His willing and wholehearted holy self-offering He opened the way for us to see the salvation of God, His Father. We respond with total gratitude and surrendered faith. 'It is not our sacrifice that tells but our union with the sacrifice of Christ which is the sacrifice of God.'[72]

If I give my body to be burned it counts for little in love except it be kindled by a spark from the all-consuming fire of His cross. The burnt offerings of our worship and ministry are merely coals on the altar of His sacrifice. His first word is judgment; thankfully, His last word is salvation.

Prayer and Reflections

Lord, I bring You my thank-offering.
The more I think of You, Lord, the more I thank You.
If the forgiven much, love much, then You deserve all my love.
Lord, I have often prayed desperate prayers. You have heard me and consoled me and acted to rescue me.
I was lost and You found me; I was in a pit I had dug for myself and You lifted me out.
I was dead and You restored me to life.
I cannot thank You enough.
Go on reclaiming my life, I pray.
Go on redeeming me Lord, and so bring me into the fullness of my intended value.
Keep me as free as love can make me.
Thank You that Your covenant love refuses to let me go and will never let me down.
Thank You that You cannot love me more than You do and will never love me less!
All my heart rejoices in You, Lord.
I offer these prayers with a grateful heart,
Amen.

- Make a list of crises from which people are saved and delivered, and describe how they might feel afterwards. What might this tell us about our worship?

- Recall the ways in which God has blessed you from your conversion onwards. Can you share with the hymnwriter, Isaac Watts, in the 'joy of sins forgiven, of hell subdued, and peace with heaven'?

- In the light of Psalm 50, why might the familiar statement – 'God has no hands but our hands to do his work' – be an inadequate reflection on God's resourcefulness and ability, and His delight in loving us?

• I thank You today for _____

WINTER SONGS

Winter Songs: Overture

Faith in a Minor Key! (Psalm 22)

Repentant Praise (Psalm 51)

Face this Way Lord (Psalm 80)

Do it Again Lord (Psalm 85)

PSALMS

'the winter of our discontent ...'

Artistic perfection takes your breath away.

I recall an evening in Portsmouth Guildhall when, as a young man, I was taken by my future father-in-law to hear the incomparable Ella Fitzgerald sing in concert with the jazz pianist Oscar Peterson and his trio: 'Blue Moon', 'Manhattan', 'Every Time We Say Goodbye' ... all the classic standards. For both of us it was a sublime night. The superb performance of all concerned could not have been bettered. It was deeply moving.

What gave such depth and poignancy to such essentially popular music and singing was, of course, its roots in the classic blues tradition. The dictionary blandly defines the blues as 'slow, sad, folksongs'. Singing the blues is singing in the tough times. Further back in cultural tradition are songs in the same mood which were directed to God, the 'spirituals' that were squeezed out of the agony of slavery in the Southern States of America.

Behind all this lies the ancient tradition of lament.

Laments are the polar opposite on the emotional spectrum to songs of cheerful and uninhibited praise. Here the psalmists give voice to hurt, and grief, shame and fear, doubt, and despair, anger and revenge. Laments are cries from the depths of sorrow or distress. They represent the dark night of the soul. Individuals sing them when illness strikes, injustice oppresses, guilt stains the conscience, or when alienation orphans the heart from what it treasures most (eg Psa. 22, 32, 51). Communal laments reflect times of national emergency, invasion or exile (eg Psa. 12, 74, 80, 85).

The most basic structure of a lament includes the following features:

- an address or cry to God for help (22:1; 74:1)
- a complaint that may include an imprecatory element
- a curse on one's enemies (22:2,6–7,11; 74:4–11)
- a confession of trust (22:3–5,9; 74:12–17)

- a petition for rescue (22:11,19; 74:18–23)
- a vow of subsequent praise (22:22,25; 74:21)
- an assurance of being heard (22:24–31; 74:20–22).

Why do we need the songs of laments?

We need laments because we need a way of dealing with strong negative emotions. The choices are few. Either we suppress the pain, which is psychologically harmful, or we vent it on others, which is socially destructive.

There is another way. We can express them honestly and fiercely to God. This is precisely what the lament prayers of the Psalms allow – indeed encourage – us to do. Evidently the psalmists believed that God had a great shock-absorbing heart. They sensed His love well enough to believe that He could cope with their most outlandish questions, unreasonable doubts, and even angriest cries for vengeance. They discovered that this was best done under the controlled conditions of ritual and liturgy.

We need such a liturgical outlet if only to keep our worship honest and in line with the reality of life as we know it.

Martin Marty even suggests there is a type of 'wintry spirituality' that fits some people's melancholic personality.[73] He insists that the winter of the soul is not a periodic mood. 'Winter, here, is a dimension of all reality, not one-fourth of the spiritual year's endless recurrings.'[74]

To recognise that the basis of life is tragic, is to preserve worship from artificial sweetness. At its best, summer praise is artless, direct, ingenuous, pure and unfeigned in its delight and joy. At its worst, such praise can become unrealistic and smug. It amounts to a fair-weather spirituality, a form of ambient music to chill out to, but not one to warm the soul by in cold times. Without the tang of wintry spirituality, worship becomes Country-and-Western.

But the Psalms are songs for all seasons. They embrace the

extremities of life, and occupy both the heights of praise and the depths of lament, encompassing what Paul Ricoeur called 'limit experiences'.[75]

Contrition confession of sin and the recognition of guilt in seeking pardon from God.

Complaint more than a rehearsal of dark feelings but a protest against the action or seeming inaction of God and a challenge to God to live up to His promises and character!

Catharsis a way of purifying the emotions by releasing them into God's keeping.

Cursing the invoking of curses upon one's enemies, usually in violent language.

Since it is this fourth category that many people find intolerable in the Psalms, we may venture a word on it.

Imprecation

What can we make of those songs where the psalmist in the full flood of feeling calls down wrath on his enemies, even, in the most notorious case, wanting his opponents' children smashed against rocks (Psa. 137:9)? Should we excise them from the Canon of Scripture, as we have eliminated them from polite worship?

Firstly, there is an undoubted cathartic value. 'In the Imprecatory Psalms,' says Miroslav Volf, 'the torrents of rage have been allowed to flow freely, channeled only by the robust structure of ritual prayer'. But of what value is this? 'Strangely enough,' argues Volf of such psalms:

they point to a way out of the slavery of hate to the freedom of forgiveness. For the followers of the crucified Messiah their main message is; hate belongs before God, not in a reflectively managed and manicured form of confession, but as a pre-reflective outburst from the depths of our being.[76]

Larry Silva has argued that the use of the lament psalms by harshly oppressed people can be a way of exorcising the demonic power of the rage they feel.[77] Remote from such raw pain, we can only feel embarrassed by such vitriolic and vituperative language.

Secondly, the release of such feelings in the controlled environment of prayer is not only a form of catharsis, a letting off of steam, it may also be the first move in a prophetic protest which needs to be made. Larry Silva explains:

> If the imprecations are used properly, recognizing that they are only a part of the complex message of the Bible and are not the last word, they can release an energy in the community that can give it courage in the midst of struggle and a sense that God understands even their darkest and most dangerous emotions – and can transform them into the true love of enemies in the achievement of justice.[78]

Imprecation can serve then as a focus for genuine prophetic protest against evil and injustice, a way of channelling the rage the powerless feel against their oppressors. By turning even anger into prayer we may achieve a spiritual and emotional alchemy. In doing so we remind ourselves brashly and boldly that divine retribution is called for on the powers-that-be – in the case of Psalm 137, the Babylonians. The downfall of evil can in the end only cause the righteous to rejoice (Rev. 19).

Thirdly, the fact that such hostile feelings are being channelled into prayer suggests they are being submitted to God and subsumed under His wider purposes of justice and mercy. In this way, as Ellen

Davis points out, 'even while we are still in our anger, the cursing psalms are the vehicle whereby we yield to God our own claim to vengeance, and that is the first step to the healing of the entire community'.[79]

This is perhaps the best that we can say, and all that we can say, about the imprecatory psalms, until we allow them to drive us to the cross where the Violated Victim absorbs all hate and violence, and turns it back on His enemies in forgiving grace.

Whatever can or cannot be said in favour of the psalms of imprecation, there is no doubt of the positive value of laments in general.

Laments re-evaluated

- Laments undermine the idea that life with God is a stress-free stroll in the park!
- Laments enable us to burden God with our negative emotions rather than poison our souls by internalising them, or misusing other people by treating them as emotional garbage cans.
- Lament is the crucial safety-valve that allows Israel's worship to breathe honesty and integrity.
- Lament penetrates to new depths of God's sensitivity and grace. Without lament, we deprive ourselves of such life-changing new encounters with God.
- Laments have dropped out of the modern liturgical repertoire, a process accentuated by the demise of psalm singing.

The absence of lament in contemporary worship practices is a great loss. It closes off one avenue of healing for those in pain and grief. It misses an opportunity for solidarity, which would build fellowship and promote brother–sister love. Moreover, it prevents worshippers breaking through to a new appreciation of and experience of God.

Should we impose laments on those who are enjoying being well-orientated?

Yes, for the following reasons:

Laments remind us of our gratitude for our own salvation when disorientated.

They prepare us in a more honest way for the prospect of future suffering.

They offer a curriculum of suffering to educate us in sympathy with those who are in distress.

They connect us in intercessory empathy with the suffering people of God around the world.[80]

Winter songs are important, then, in keeping our worship practices connected to the jagged-edged reality of our experience. 'Covenant minus lament,' advises Walter Brueggemann, 'is finally a practice of denial, cover-up and pretence, which sanctions social control.'[81]

Allowing wintry spirituality its place may be, surprisingly, the catalyst for change. The autumn leaves tell us that only God can make dying things beautiful. Winter in the soul may be the vital purgation and necessary death that enables new life to spring forth.

Faith in a Minor Key! (Psalm 22)

For the director of music. To the tune of 'The Doe of the Morning'. A psalm of David.

[1]My God, my God, why have you forsaken me?
  Why are you so far from saving me,
  so far from the words of my groaning?
[2]O my God, I cry out by day, but you do not answer,
  by night, and am not silent.

³Yet you are enthroned as the Holy One;
  you are the praise of Israel.
⁴In you our fathers put their trust;
  they trusted and you delivered them.
⁵They cried to you and were saved;
  in you they trusted and were not disappointed.

⁶But I am a worm and not a man,
  scorned by men and despised by the people.
⁷All who see me mock me;
  they hurl insults, shaking their heads:
⁸ 'He trusts in the LORD;
  let the LORD rescue him.
Let him deliver him,
  since he delights in him.'

⁹Yet you brought me out of the womb;
  you made me trust in you
  even at my mother's breast.
¹⁰From birth I was cast upon you;
  from my mother's womb you have been my God.
¹¹Do not be far from me,
  for trouble is near
  and there is no-one to help.

¹²Many bulls surround me;
  strong bulls of Bashan encircle me.
¹³Roaring lions tearing their prey
  open their mouths wide against me.
¹⁴I am poured out like water,
  and all my bones are out of joint.
My heart has turned to wax;
  it has melted away within me.
¹⁵My strength is dried up like a potsherd,

and my tongue sticks to the roof of my mouth;
you lay me in the dust of death.
[16]Dogs have surrounded me;
a band of evil men has encircled me,
they have pierced my hands and my feet.
[17]I can count all my bones;
people stare and gloat over me.
[18]They divide my garments among them
and cast lots for my clothing.

[19]But you, O LORD, be not far off;
O my Strength, come quickly to help me.
[20]Deliver my life from the sword,
my precious life from the power of the dogs.
[21]Rescue me from the mouth of the lions;
save me from the horns of the wild oxen.

[22]I will declare your name to my brothers;
in the congregation I will praise you.
[23]You who fear the LORD, praise him!
All you descendants of Jacob, honour him!
Revere him, all you descendants of Israel!
[24]For he has not despised or disdained
the suffering of the afflicted one;
he has not hidden his face from him
but has listened to his cry for help.

[25]From you comes the theme of my praise in the great assembly;
before those who fear you will I fulfil my vows.
[26]The poor will eat and be satisfied;
they who seek the LORD will praise him –
may your hearts live for ever!
[27]All the ends of the earth
will remember and turn to the LORD,

and all the families of the nations
  will bow down before him,
[28]for dominion belongs to the LORD
  and he rules over the nations.

[29]All the rich of the earth will feast and worship;
  all who go down to the dust will kneel before him –
  those who cannot keep themselves alive.
[30]Posterity will serve him;
  future generations will be told about the LORD.
[31]They will proclaim his righteousness
  to a people yet unborn –
  for he has done it.

THIS SONG IS TRULY A CASE OF INTRUDING ON PRIVATE grief.

It is an anguished individual lament.

The singer is fighting for faith like a suffocating person fights for breath.

Like a drowning man coming up for air, he surfaces with three stark negatives as he clutches at three straws of faith:

- No answer given (v.2)
- No humanity left (v.6)
- No help at hand (v.11)

And 'yet ... and yet ... and yet ...' (vv.3, 9, 19)!

All these can be heard in the solo voice as it pours out its lament (vv.1–21).

What we are told first (vv.1–5) is that the psalmist feels *spiritually abandoned* and there is no answer (v.2).

To be rejected, abandoned, left behind, cast aside, forsaken – these are the bitterest of all human experiences. The cruel isolation is compounded by the feeling that God has turned His back, and moved away out of sight and out of earshot. The once-beckoning heavens are as brass. Our bleeding knuckles beat at a bolted door that no one can open.

And 'yet …'! When all five senses lose touch with reality, numbed by grief and despair, a spiritual sixth sense hangs on to plead with God. The God who has forsaken him is nevertheless being addressed! And He is being addressed still as 'my God'. Here is a God who even in His seeming absence can be questioned and pressed for a reason.

'Why … why have you forsaken me?'

Never be afraid to ask God 'why?' never be afraid to ask God anything. He is unshockable.

So the psalmist pleads from memory of the sovereignty of this God who is enthroned amidst His people's praise. This may reflect the fact that in the Tabernacle and, later, in the Temple, God was said to be enthroned above the mercy seat of the ark of the covenant which was deemed to be – the earthly footstool of His heavenly throne. The psalmist pleads, not only the sovereign power of God but the holiness of God (v.3) by invoking the name for God so often used by the prophet Isaiah – 'the Holy One' of Israel. Then the psalmist argues from God's history with His people (vv.4–5), as if playing his last card: 'You did it before to the forefathers in the faith; do it again now, Lord.'

The psalmist is spiritually bereft, plunged into darkness, abandoned and alone. But surely God is in control; God is holy; God has a track record of salvation. Theology is here on its knees wrestling with the brute facts of experience!

But there is more. The psalmist tells us that he feels *emotionally overwhelmed* – a worm and not a man (v.6).

Such expressions are often parodied as 'worm theology' and the Church is mocked for having a stake in self-deprecation and in perpetuating a view of humans as 'miserable offenders'. Winston Churchill poked fun at this attitude by saying, 'I may be a worm but I am a glow-worm!' But responses like this are reactions to a caricature. The psalmist's confession is not some phony 'Uriah Heep type' of false modesty. This is a soul in extremis! It indicates dying or the imminence of death. His condition is so dire he feels he has lost his humanity altogether.

This is 'Auschwitz man' who has lost all sense of being a human being at all. Even in its milder forms this social alienation is painful. The loss of self-esteem, the awareness of being marginalised, the acute sense of being an outsider, looking in from the outside on to the charmed inner circle.

The last insult to offer such a person in such a condition is to say: 'Just praise the Lord' (see v.7). It is the worst kind of mockery to a sufferer like this to throw pious platitudes at him from a safe distance, bombard him or her with texts in a futile effort to induce faith. When God is silent only Christian fools rush in to do a PR job for Him; the angels are more circumspect. In any case it is always a futile exercise to attempt to get people to believe by telling them to believe or by preaching faith to them. Better to put them back in touch with a God they cannot help believing in.

'Yet ...' (v.9), just as his self-despair threatens to engulf him, he recalls his deep roots in God. He realises he has not fallen right to the bottom of the pit but is clinging very precariously to a narrow ledge of memory. Faith is hanging on by its fingertips, as the psalmist recalls the moments when he was most vulnerable and most dependent and reflects that from within his mother's womb, God has been his God (vv.9–10)! The incidence of abortion virtually on demand means that the unborn are now most at risk from their own mothers. Thankfully, our psalmist had a godly mother who conceived and carried him in faith, bore him with praise to the Lord and Giver of Life, and nurtured him in the faith of his fathers.

What came from the womb was not a worm but a person made in God's image. Its destiny was not to be victimised and trampled underfoot as a sub-human species but to be received with dignity and respect – even by us!

The psalmist is not yet finished. As well as being spiritually abandoned and emotionally overwhelmed, he confesses to being *physically broken* and there is no one to help (vv.11–21).

The language here is graphic. Was the psalmist sick? Perhaps, as Peter Craigie suggests, this psalm may have been used as part of a liturgy for healing in the community.

The pressure he feels is certainly vividly described. It is like being surrounded by: charging bulls (v.12), ravening lions (v.13), vicious dogs (v.16). He feels trapped, ambushed, hemmed in. The effects in his body are drastic. Notice the pains he feels: he is utterly enervated, washed out like water (v.14); his aching bones torn apart as with a severe fever (v.14). He feels as weak as putty or wax (v.14b); shattered like a piece of broken pottery (v.15). Absolute terror dries up his mouth (v.15b)! How vivid and true to life is his description.

'But ...' having said all this he still pleads God's saving strength (vv.19–21). Above all, he longs to be reassured and healed by God's nearness: 'Do not be far from me ... O LORD, be not far off' (vv.11, 19).

At this point comes a turning-point in the psalmist's personal drama. The whole mood of the song changes. Somewhere between verses 21 and 22 the psalmist gets his answer (see v.24c). Perhaps an answer came through prophetic oracle interjected into worship! Perhaps a priest brought immediate assurance of answered prayer. Whatever way God's answer comes, the psalmist hears and receives it. Which raises the passing question: do we listen enough in prayer or worship? Is it possible to be so absorbed in singing songs as to miss the voice of God itself? Can we praise away the presence of God?

However it has occurred, the psalm is now transformed from lament to praise (vv.22–31). *Faith can now sing in the major key!*

The jubilant psalmist first addresses God (v.22), 'I will declare your name to my brothers; in the congregation I will praise you.' So the happy psalmist pledges to be a leading worshipper, to make notable his thanks by publicly praising the name of the Lord his benefactor.

Next, he addresses the congregation, 'You who fear the Lord, praise him!' (v.23). Eagerly he calls on others to join him in what God has inspired (vv.23–25). His recruits for the praise of the kingdom include: sufferers (v.24), seekers (v.26), all the ends of the earth (v.27), the poor (v.26) and the prosperous (v.29), the dying (v.29b), the living (v.30) and the unborn (v.31) – all are persuaded to join the universal, age-long, ever-expanding circle of praise. This cross-generational, worldwide chorus of praise celebrates that 'dominion belongs to the Lord' (v.28).

Without embarking on an undue 'Christianising' of this psalm, no one can fail to trace the trajectory of this poignant song all the way to the cross. Jesus sang this song in extreme anguish (Matt. 27:46).

One psalmist's grief became a Saviour's dereliction. Only broken fragments of song passed His parched lips but by-standers heard Him croak the first words: 'My God ... why have you forsaken me?' and the last: 'It is finished' (John 19:30; Psa. 22:31).

Those who overheard this crucified man, battered beyond all human recognition, were perhaps the first to begin dimly to perceive the mystery of His cross: that beneath what was being endured something was being done, that His agony and abandonment was in fact masking a momentous achievement!

Not surprisingly, Christian liturgical tradition has seen a sequence in the Psalm collection:

from Psalm 22 speaking of crucifixion,
to Psalm 23 of resurrection,
and Psalm 24 of ascension and exaltation.

According to the writer to the Hebrews, Jesus sings this song still in the assembly of all who rejoice in His suffering and achievement (Heb. 2:12). What an extraordinary insight. In our worship and praise Jesus is leading the singing!

Charles Spurgeon asked:

Is Jesus as man ... the great leader of the devotion of the skies? Is he the chief musician of the sky? Does he beat time for all the hallelujahs of the universe? I think so. In the midst of the congregation on earth, too, Jesus Christ is the sweetest of singers. Is not Jesus Christ in the midst of the congregation, gathering up all the notes which come from sincere lips to put them into his golden censer and to make them rise as precious incense before the throne ... so that He is the great singer, rather than we? He is the chief player on our stringed instruments, the great master of the music. The worship of earth comes up to God through Him and He is the accepted channel of all the praise of all the redeemed universe.[82]

Paul rehearsed the story of Jesus as culminating in a solo voice declaring: 'I will praise you among the Gentiles; I will sing hymns to your name' (Rom. 15:9), on which James Denney commented that 'Christ is assumed to be the speaker and we may say that he gives thanks to God among the gentiles when the gentiles give thanks to God through him'.

The famous devotional writer and preacher, F.B. Meyer, struck a similar note when he said that 'Whenever in a great congregation of saints there is an outburst of divine song, you may detect the voice of Jesus singing with them and identifying himself with it.'

It is from such depths of despair and agony as Psalm 22 represents that such exalted sentiments arise.

The implications for our praise are profound. The more realistic the lament, the more honest the praise. Only the weight of deeper experiences will raise the quality of our worship, especially His experience! For the stream of praise rises deep in the dark hillside of Calvary. Out of the hidden depths of His darkest hour, flows the river of our richest praise. Because He has shared our bitterest laments, and carried our sins and griefs in His own body to the tree, we can be the outlet for His worship, and the mouth-piece for His victory song.

Repentant Praise (Psalm 51)

For the director of music. A psalm of David. When the prophet Nathan came to him after David had committed adultery with Bathsheba.

[1]Have mercy on me, O God,
   according to your unfailing love;
according to your great compassion
   blot out my transgressions.
[2]Wash away all my iniquity
   and cleanse me from my sin.

[3]For I know my transgressions,
   and my sin is always before me.
[4]Against you, you only, have I sinned
   and done what is evil in your sight,
so that you are proved right when you speak
   and justified when you judge.
[5]Surely I was sinful at birth,
   sinful from the time my mother conceived me.
[6]Surely you desire truth in the inner parts;
   you teach me wisdom in the inmost place.

[7]Cleanse me with hyssop, and I shall be clean;
   wash me, and I shall be whiter than snow.
[8]Let me hear joy and gladness;
   let the bones you have crushed rejoice.
[9]Hide your face from my sins
   and blot out all my iniquity.

[10]Create in me a pure heart, O God,
  and renew a steadfast spirit within me.
[11]Do not cast me from your presence
  or take your Holy Spirit from me.
[12]Restore to me the joy of your salvation
  and grant me a willing spirit, to sustain me.
[13]Then I will teach transgressors your ways,
  and sinners will turn back to you.
[14]Save me from bloodguilt, O God,
  the God who saves me,
  and my tongue will sing of your righteousness.
[15]O Lord, open my lips,
  and my mouth will declare your praise.
[16]You do not delight in sacrifice, or I would bring it;
  you do not take pleasure in burnt offerings.
[17]The sacrifices of God are a broken spirit;
  a broken and contrite heart,
  O God, you will not despise.

[18]In your good pleasure make Zion prosper;
  build up the walls of Jerusalem.
[19]Then there will be righteous sacrifices,
  whole burnt offerings to delight you;
  then bulls will be offered on your altar.

PALAEONTOLOGISTS HAVE AN EASIER TIME BEING TRENDY than preachers do with the subject of this psalm: sin. This is odd, to say the least. Evidence for the condition screams at us from every tabloid headline and glares out at us from every TV news story. It even stares back at us from the bathroom mirror. But no one will use the 's' word. It is the unlove that dares not speak its name. Both socially and personally, there is a conspiracy of silence over sin. We are all in denial here. But why the massive cover-up? The reason for this, says theologian Ted Peters, is deceit.

Inherent in sin is the denial of truth. We cover over unwholesome motives and violent acts against others with a veneer of goodness. We sugarcoat our garbage. Everyone has a stake in hiding the truth of sin. This makes uncovering the truth of how sin works difficult, because wherever we dig, lies rush in to fill the hole.[83]

'Perhaps the only way to get at the truth of sin,' Peters suggests, 'is through confession.' Confession of sin is precisely what this great penitential Psalm 51 offers us. The psalmist begins by casting himself upon the mercy of God. He pleads God's steadfast and unfailing love ('*hesed*'). He does not come looking for a therapist to help him feel better about himself; but he does trust that God is not unfeeling and that, in His compassion, God will understand Him better than he does himself. This is the decisive move. Just such a move triggered the Reformation as Martin Luther asked: 'Where can I find a gracious God?'

In the first half of his prayer, the psalmist confesses to an ever-deepening awareness of the depths and ramifications of his sinfulness (vv.1–9). The synonyms pile up as he admits his 'sin', that tragic missing of the mark of God's calling for our lives. Sin causes us to fall short of the glorious destiny God has for us within His will. 'Transgression' ('*abar*', vv.1,3) exposes sin as rebellion. To transgress is to cross over into forbidden territory, to infringe the God-given limitations on our lives, to break the rules that safeguard our freedom, to defy the 'Maker's instructions' for how human life works best. So we are law-breakers, rebels caught with the weapons of insurrection in our hands.

But even this is only a symptom of a deeper problem. The springs of our personality have been poisoned at source. We have no need to resort to later definitions of 'total depravity' to recognise our 'iniquity' ('*avon*', vv.2,5) – that fatal twist, the warped heart, which lying deep within us perverts truth into lies, and corrupts even good intentions into acts of disobedience.

Deeper than sins is sin

Transgressions are external acts that God in His mercy may 'blot out' from His record book (v.1).

My deep-seated iniquity only God can 'wash out' (vv.2,7). Only God can do this because, in the end, all sin is 'against' Him. 'All sin is sacrilege,' said C.S. Lewis, 'for every sin is the distortion of an energy breathed into us.'[84]

Let's assume for a moment that this confession was a hand-me-down from David's adulterous failure with Bathsheba and subsequent involvement in the death of her husband. What had he done? He had despoiled the temple which was Bathsheba's beauty, desecrated the sanctuary which was Uriah's trust and the couple's faithfulness, and profaned his own high, holy and royally human calling before God. So we prostitute our God-given gifts and fail in our sacred stewardship of life. In Emil Brunner's words, 'The wine of the divine love has become the vinegar of enmity towards God.'[85]

So the psalmist is brought to realise that not only does he commit sin, he is a sinner. Sin has to do with what we are not just what we do: 'sinful from the time my mother conceived me ...' (v.5). This puts to rest the myth of the angelic baby. We all arrive damaged goods. We suffer psychological trauma in the womb. We are conceived in and born into a web of imperfect relationships and motivation. Original sin has been resisted as too deterministic. Yet increasingly we talk of crime as caused by social deprivation. Daily we face a battle with addictions of all kinds which seem to have robbed people of choice and made them victims. Now we grapple with theories of genetic evolution that sound equally threatening to human freedom. Paradoxically, as Ted Peters notes,

we find ourselves in the curious situation in which Christian theologians affirm the notion of original sin but are reluctant to affirm its biological transmissibility, whereas natural scientists are debating the possibility that human predispositions towards what hitherto has been known as sinful behaviour is genetically inherited.[86]

However we construe the twists and turns of sin, the problem is deep with in us. 'Create in me a pure heart, O God' is therefore the key prayer (v.10). It is 'our inner parts' that are the danger-zone (v.6).

Inner space is the unconquered frontier. Sin is not a surface problem to which we can apply a religious cosmetic but trouble in the 'inmost place', in the hidden recesses of our personality. Heart trouble needs heart surgery and a heart transplant!

Sin is *unreality* (v.6), the loss of inner truth, so that we become self-deceived. Our sinful self feeds on lies, heeds false voices, breeds falsehood, and indulges in fantasy. The psalmist prays for integrity, where what you see is what you get. He pleads for the spiritual wisdom that only God can give.

He confesses his *uncleanness* (v.10). Anticipating Jesus, he begins to realise that it is not what goes into a person but what comes out of a person that defiles. So he prays for purity of mind and motive. He asks to be made clean and uncomplicated and focused in what he devotes his energies to.

'Purity of heart is to will one thing' (Kierkegaard). Here is a plea for cleansing from mixed motives, and double-mindedness (see James 4:8).

In asking 'renew a steadfast spirit within me ', the psalmist is asking for his *unreliability* to be redressed (v.10). What got him into so much sin was precisely the tendency to live off feelings and moods rather than principles and convictions. He acknowledges he has been erratic and inconsistent. The psalmist would have agreed with the sage who said: 'Like a city whose walls are broken down is a man who lacks self-control' (Prov. 25:28). So he prays for a spirit-controlled temperament, to be steadfast, committed and reliable.

He confronts his *unspirituality* (v.11). To have the Spirit of God but to quench, resist or insult Him is to risk losing the Spirit. The psalmist lacks nothing in religious pedigree but mourns the loss of the sense of God's presence. Has the psalmist sinned because he has been over-familiar with God's Spirit, failing to recognise His lordship and neglecting to rely on Him? Amazingly, the Spirit has stayed with him through it all. Whatever the reason, he repentantly prays not to be deprived of the Holy Spirit. The Holy Spirit is the indispensable requirement, as King David had once known (1 Sam. 16:13).

As Walter Brueggemann comments:

> ... in his unthinkable act against Uriah and Bathsheba, David has lost the power of Yahweh authorising him to rule. The wind to govern is gladly given by Yahweh but it is never possessed. It is always held in trust ...
>
> Such utterly alien sin can leave us powerless and without authority for living our lives. So David asks for a re-issue of gifts that make a regal life possible.[87]

The psalmist confesses to an *unwillingess* of spirit (v.12). An 'unwilling' spirit is a heart and mind unengaged with God, emotionally in neutral gear. I suspect that David was bored when he looked over at Bathsheba. And, as Kierkegaard said: 'boredom is the root of all evil'. Urban crime levels confirm his view. The craving for excitement fuels drug addiction and violence by those who protest, 'We're bored: there's nothing to do'. Boredom is the kiss of death; wonder is the beginning of wisdom. All the psalms seek to inspire this. Even the lament psalms we are considering implicitly warn us against dampening down our emotional fires, of numbing our senses. We are warned against the withholding of ourselves in relationships with others or with God in worship. Sin makes us sullen and unforthcoming, joyless (v.12) and withdrawn. Forgiveness restores joy and releases praise. So he prays to be, as Derek Kidner suggests, an enthusiastic volunteer.[88]

Stoicism is not the way to avoid sinning: 'No soul is pure that is not passionate ...' So the psalmist asks to be 'sustained' in and by his eagerness.

The psalmist's unravelling of his innermost self shows that he is ready to be broken open, to be vulnerable. He will not retreat behind what have been called 'walls of appropriateness', even if they be worship itself (v.16). The singer has abandoned all self-protective devices to embrace openness.

He spells out the lesson he is learning. 'The sacrifices of God are a broken spirit; a broken and contrite heart, O God, you will not despise' (v.17). As Ellen Davis puts it, this is a 'voluntary heartbreak'.[89] It makes the whole psalm, concludes James Mays, 'a liturgy of the broken heart'.[90]

All this is a prayer for new covenant realities: for deep forgiveness; for a heart-transplant which replaces a hard heart with a soft, responsive one, programmed to obey God with joy and delight; for the presence and power of God's Spirit within and for restoration of intimacy with God (Jer. 33; Ezek. 36).

Grace is a moral miracle, and other signs follow those who receive it.

Towards God there is a renewed and greater freedom (vv.14–15). Tongues are loosed and praise is released from its shackles. The heart that has been opened to divine inspection and grace leads to a mouth open in praise.

Towards others there is a new openness (v.13). When truth is re-established on the inside, the anointing to teach and mentor others is restored. Humbly now, and with greater vulnerability than before, we can bear testimony to grace and become enthusiastic worshippers and authentic witnesses again.

The transformation of the individual penitent helps to rebuild the community of God (vv.18–19). These verses tell against the idea that the psalm is an anti-sacrificial polemic. Even if they were added later after the Exile, they only reinforce the original singer's view. 'Sacrifices offered from vain hearts are sacrifices in vain.'[91] It is not difficult to see how, on the return from exile, the 'I' of verses 1–17 could serve in a corporate sense, expressing the whole community's penitence and faith. Confession is good for the soul of every community.

Why then do pastors and worship leaders camouflage confession? According to Kathleen Norris: 'One week, the confession began: "Our communication with Jesus tends to be too infrequent to experience the transformation in our lives You want us to have", which seems less a prayer than a memo from one professional to another.' 'At such times,' Norris adds, 'I picture God as a wily writing teacher who leans across the table and says, not at all gently, "Could you possibly be troubled to say what you mean?" It would be refreshing to answer simply, 'I have sinned.'[92]

Our life with God – to use a phrase of P.T. Forsyth's – is a life of 'repentant praise'. Of the returning prodigal now home again, he wrote:

> But can I sit mute in my Father's house?
> Or remember without amaze?
> Can I ever live but to bless thee and serve,
> And the deeper to grieve in praise?[93]

'What sweeter music shall we bring?' – to use Robert Herrick's words – what sweeter music shall we bring than the bitter joy of repentant praise?

Face this Way Lord (Psalm 80)

For the director of music. To the tune of 'The Lilies of the Covenant'. Of Asaph. A psalm.

[1]Hear us, O Shepherd of Israel,
    you who lead Joseph like a flock;
you who sit enthroned between the cherubim, shine forth
[2]before Ephraim, Benjamin and Manasseh.

Awaken your might;
   come and save us.

³Restore us, O God;
   make your face shine upon us,
   that we may be saved.

⁴O Lᴏʀᴅ God Almighty,
   how long will your anger smoulder
   against the prayers of your people?
⁵You have fed them with the bread of tears;
   you have made them drink tears by the bowlful.
⁶You have made us a source of contention to our neighbours,
   and our enemies mock us.

⁷Restore us, O God Almighty;
   make your face shine upon us,
   that we may be saved.

⁸You brought a vine out of Egypt;
   you drove out the nations and planted it.
⁹You cleared the ground for it,
   and it took root and filled the land.
¹⁰The mountains were covered with its shade,
   the mighty cedars with its branches.
¹¹It sent out its boughs to the Sea,
   its shoots as far as the River.

¹²Why have you broken down its walls
   so that all who pass by pick its grapes?
¹³Boars from the forest ravage it
   and the creatures of the field feed on it.
¹⁴Return to us, O God Almighty!
   Look down from heaven and see!

Watch over this vine,
[15] the root your right hand has planted,
the son you have raised up for yourself.
[16]Your vine is cut down, it is burned with fire;
at your rebuke your people perish.
[17]Let your hand rest on the man at your right hand,
the son of man you have raised up for yourself.
[18]Then we will not turn away from you;
revive us, and we will call on your name.

[19]Restore us, O LORD God Almighty;
make your face shine upon us,
that we may be saved.

WHEN DID YOU LAST HEAR A LAMENT IN YOUR CHURCH?
Psalm 80 is a 'community lament' – a cry of anguish from God's
people grieved by their own failure and God's seeming absence.
Three out of ten psalms are laments which far outnumber any other
kind of songs in the Psalter.

None of this is too well represented in our contemporary
songbooks! The upsurge of praise among us is welcome but too
often it is at the expense of prayer. In non-liturgical churches at
least, supplication and petition have been all but swept aside by the
tide of rejoicing, while penitential songs have sunk without trace
beneath a flood of over-confident celebration. Subtly lulled into a
sense of self-satisfaction, we stay complacent over the state of the
Church, and parochial in the scope of our concern. But 'community
lament' lies at the heart of intercession and of our plea for revival.
And we need to re-learn how to pray like Psalm 80: 'Restore us, O
God; make your face shine upon us, that we may be saved'
(vv.3,7,19). This refrain is the keynote, marking out three stanzas in
this song.

Making a complaint from within the covenant relationship is
the heart of a lament! Complaining to God is an unabashed feature

of Israel's relationship with Yahweh (see Psa. 142:2). God would rather, it seems, that we rushed into His office to demand His resignation than to 'doff our caps' to Him at a respectful religious distance only to vent our rage against Him 'behind His back' before a cynical world!

Religion which is designed to protect God's sensitivities is pagan; it usually ends with the worshippers losing their sensitivity. Worship that is too compliant and never complaining is untruthful. Such worship serves only to distance a perfectionist God from the pains and questions of His troubled people. If we are never anything but wildly triumphalistic, our worship becomes sycophantic. We fawn over God rather than adore Him. Over time this slowly but surely reinforces a sense of God's indifference. When praise is perverted into flattery we have lost God for the simple reason that He doesn't need us to convince Him how wonderful He is. He prefers to show it by His grace and mercy.

Unlike the 'Narnia' of C.S. Lewis, praise God, it's not 'always winter but never Christmas'. But neither is it always Christmas and never winter – else we are left with a Santa Claus God! So within covenant, complaining, while never applauded, is at least allowed.

But this is what makes lament-within-covenant distinctive! Confidence while complaining is the mark of such laments. For the people of God even grief is different (see 1 Thess. 4:13)!

Psalms like Psalm 80 are not bemoaning a tragedy that cannot be reversed, or a fate that is inevitable. This is not just catharsis however therapeutic. With this lament goes a bold act of faith that petitions God to intervene and save. Here is faith which is not perverted into that parody of itself called 'positive thinking'. Here is true biblical faith which is able to embrace life's extreme negatives and therefore save itself from unreality. Yet this is no banging-the-head-against-the-wall futility. This is a piercing cry from the depths of profound pain for the help of a covenant God.

A lament, like Psalm 80, can therefore truly be seen as a form of praise 'in a minor key'.

(a) Psalm 80 begins by appealing to God as **the shepherd of the flock** who guides, protects and fights for His people (v.1).

Even more than in Psalm 23, the shepherd nature of God is appealed to out of crisis. 'Shepherd' neatly combines the fundamental elements of covenant and kingship which Psalms 1 and 2 introduce us to. 'Shepherd' was a regular title of kingship in the Ancient Near East. In Israel's distinctive testimony it spoke tenderness as well as toughness, sensitivity as well as authority.

God's heavenly rule is encountered at His earthly footstool – the 'ark of the covenant' – that sacred chest with carved figures of cherubim over it (v.1b) which was carried at the head of Israel across the wilderness and into the battle of the conquest of Canaan. The ark – the symbol of God's enthronement in the midst of His people – had been brought by David to Jerusalem and established there in His tent sanctuary and later by Solomon in the permanent Temple. Centuries later, when Temple and ark had long gone, its language was used still to evoke the thought of an ever present, reigning Lord operating – as Ezekiel discovered in exile – from a mobile throne room.

Bolstered by this conviction, some hard-nosed complaining is going on! 'You're not listening, Lord ... you're not awake ... you're not looking our way ... you're not doing anything, Lord!' Eugene Peterson captures the rawness of emotion here: 'Get out of bed – you've slept long enough! Come on the run before it's too late' (*The Message*).

Five urgent imperatives show the desperation: 'Hear us' (v.1a), 'shine forth' (v.1b), 'stir yourself' (v.2a), 'come and save us' (v.2b). Above all 'make your face shine upon us' (v.3).

The 'face' of God is a vivid metaphor for God's 'Presence'. When God 'hides His face' from His people, He becomes the hidden God of judgment. When He shows His face to His people it is to make Himself manifestly present to them. The outshining of God's 'face' is the standard Old Testament expression for the enjoyment of an intimate and blessed relationship with God. God's 'face' turned towards us is the shining of His favour on us. When He turns His face to us we know the beneficent nearness of God. In this stance, said R.K. Harrison: 'God is looking directly at his people so that they may receive the benefits of his full attention.'

That God should turn back to us is now the urgent need. But there is biting irony in this as verse 18 unwittingly reveals: 'Then we will not turn away from you …'

Who, in fact, had turned away from whom? Evidently, the praying of prayers had gone on unabated but only now do we wake up to the fact that God has not been listening!

Can so many prayers be prayed without expectation of God hearing them? And no doubt the liturgy had rolled on as usual, as 'lip-service' was paid to a deity with a 'do not disturb' on His door! Going through the motions of religion we are anxious to 'let sleeping gods lie'. We go about our own sweet ways until our own sweet ways turn sour on us. Suddenly it matters that God is alive and well and awake and willing to intervene!

Even seeking God's 'face' can become a formal, perfunctory business, so that we fail to notice that He has turned away. And we failed to notice that God had averted His face because the eyes of our heart were looking the other way. Now we realise He's angry with our prayers (v.4), that His 'anger smoulders against them'. Even religion, which is said to be the last refuge from God, can hide us no longer. We must have His face, whatever the shock the encounter brings.

God's people mourn their meagre diet. Fed on an unremitting diet of tears, God's people will accept no cheap remedies peddled by smooth-talking faith-merchants (v.5). Solid food not syrup is what we hunger for.

God's people have become 'a source of contention' (v.6), an object of ridicule, and poked fun at day after day. And when God's people are mocked God is demeaned. Our deep embarrassment at the humiliation of God's Church before a mocking world will not be assuaged by a glossy new brochure. Give us meat to eat not a brighter menu to admire. 'Restore us, O God Almighty ...' (v.7).

(b) Psalm 80:8–15 now appeals to God as **the 'husbandman of the vine'**: 'You brought a vine out of Egypt; you drove out the nations and planted it. You cleared the ground for it, and it took root and filled the land' (vv.8–9).

God was the gardener who had replanted His people Israel displaced from Egypt into the ground He had cleared for them in Canaan (vv.8–11). This image of Israel as a 'vine' is a familiar one throughout the Old Testament (see Isa. 5:1ff).

In particular, the tribe of Joseph – mentioned in verses 1–2 – that had formed the core of the Northern Kingdom of Israel since the tragic division of the nation after Solomon, had once been destined to be a 'fruitful vine' (Gen. 49:22). Now, overrun by the Assyrians in 720 BC, the once fruitful nation lies withered and ruined, ravaged and trampled on by her enemies. The supplication intensifies: 'Return to us, O God Almighty! ... Look down ... see ...' visit us again in saving grace and restoration (v.14).

The language here is characteristically bold and risky: it verges on asking God to repent! 'Turn round, Lord: turn our way.' It is like grabbing someone by the arm and forcing them to stop and take notice! The emotions are passionately expressed. Something of their forcefulness survives down the centuries even as this psalm was adapted for liturgical worship and prayed at different crises during Israel's long story. Standing back a little we can summarise how – by the end of the psalm – the motives for praying for revival are now purified and made clearer.

In the first place (vv.1–6) the grieving people plead *a sense of 'shame'*. Here we overhear them appealing to God's own 'reputation' as Moses had done centuries before (Exod. 32:11–14). Moses pleaded: 'What will the neighbours think?' and 'Don't you deserve a return on your investment?' Even if we use more refined language, this is still the heart of a plea for revival.

'These are the motives in praying for revival. For the name, and honour, and glory of God and for the sake of the church which is His.'[94] God's reputation is at stake before a cynical and unbelieving world.

In the next stanza (vv.7–15), the singers argue *from a sense of 'history'*. The worshippers appeal to the huge investment God has made in the life and story of His people. Historical perspective helps us here, especially when, longing for revival, we can look back over the long story of God's dealings with His people and take heart that in more desperate times than these God has responded to restore His people. With relief we can jettison the arrogance of thinking ourselves the 'first' generation of real Christians who ever lived, and the egotism that assumes we are the 'last' generation of believers who must 'get the job' done. God moves in long orbits. He has been building his covenant people for a long time. He is not in a hurry. A keener sense of history will give integrity and faith to our prayers for revival. This is His work! What He has begun to do He will surely bring to completion – and on this we rest our prayers and hopes.

Lastly, the lament expresses an unshakable *sense of destiny* (vv.17–18). There are echoes here of Israel's unique covenant designation as God's 'firstborn son' (Exod. 4:22–23). Verse 15 speaks of Israel as 'the root your right hand has planted, the son you have raised up for yourself'. Now the prayer is: 'Let your hand rest on the man at your right hand, the son of man you have raised up for yourself.' Israel was called God's 'son' – as the human partner in God's covenant plans. At one time these descriptions devolved upon Israel's king who embodied the nation's destiny. When kingship failed and Israel was exiled where do these hopes and dreams go? Is there any future? Does the son get to gain his inheritance?

Here is a muted appeal to that longed-for messianic climax of God's journey with His people. From our vantage point, this side of Christmas and Easter we can afford to be less muted and more robust in our prayer. We confidently pin our hopes on the One and only Son who embodied all that Israel was intended to be, who proved God's faithful covenant partner. We expectantly base our prayers on the ultimate Son of Man, who visited the wasteland as the sacrificial Good Shepherd of God's flock, as the True Vine whose resurrection sap is in us to revitalise and bring forth fruit.

'Let us live that we may call upon your name' – since the concern for God's glory which is the starting-point of revival is at the same time the established result of revival.

Psalm 80 may have originated in the dark days of Israel's absorption into Assyrian tyranny. Very unusually it was sung in the Southern Kingdom of Judah, and survived beyond Judah's own exile in the songbook of the Second Temple. Is this not intercession, to lament in solidarity with that part of God's people undergoing oppression, to weep with those who mourn in other parts of our world, as well as to rejoice with those who stand beside us every Sunday morning? These three combine to prompt the cry for revival:

- a sense of shame
- a sense of history
- a sense of destiny

But the greatest of these is love; love for God's name, for God's people, for God's future.

Love for God's name, and honour and reputation ...

Love for God's people, their privileged history and unique responsibility ...

Love for God's future, for the promises He has made and intends to keep, for the inheritance He has destined to His right-hand man, Jesus ...

This love is what constrains us to pray:

Yahweh, God of the angel armies, come back! Smile your blessing smile: that will be salvation (*The Message*).

Do it Again Lord (Psalm 85)

For the director of music. Of the Sons of Korah. A psalm.

[1]You showed favour to your land, O LORD;
   you restored the fortunes of Jacob.
[2]You forgave the iniquity of your people
   and covered all their sins.   *Selah*
[3]You set aside all your wrath
   and turned from your fierce anger.

[4]Restore us again, O God our Saviour,
   and put away your displeasure towards us.
[5]Will you be angry with us for ever?
   Will you prolong your anger through all generations?
[6]Will you not revive us again,
   that your people may rejoice in you?
[7]Show us your unfailing love, O LORD,
   and grant us your salvation.

[8]I will listen to what God the LORD will say;
   he promises peace to his people, his saints –
   but let them not return to folly.
[9]Surely his salvation is near those who fear him,
   that his glory may dwell in our land.

[10]Love and faithfulness meet together;
   righteousness and peace kiss each other.
[11]Faithfulness springs forth from the earth,
   and righteousness looks down from heaven.
[12]The LORD will indeed give what is good,
   and our land will yield its harvest.
[13]Righteousness goes before him
   and prepares the way for his steps.

I LOOK BACK ON MY 50 YEARS OF ACTIVE FAITH WITH immense gratitude to God for what I have seen and experienced. As a student I benefited from those Bible-believing scholars whose lonely battle with theological liberalism won them few friends in the academy but saved many thinking souls outside of it. Their brave pioneering efforts burgeoned into the stimulating and first-class evangelical scholarship we enjoy today. As a young minister I drew eagerly on the ministry of Martyn Lloyd-Jones and A.W. Tozer who deepened a desperate thirst for God in many of my generation. They were true prophets preparing the way of the Lord. Before long, the renewing work of the Holy Spirit known as 'the charismatic movement' swept us up in its tornado of joy and freedom and church-changing experiences. Renewal was followed by Restoration in which God set about reordering His Church. It was heady stuff. I wonder how far we've come?

As I look out on today's Church, half-renewed and partially restored, I sense that it would do well to pray Psalm 85.

When the first euphoria of the exiles' return from Babylon fades without them seeing all that they had hoped to see, prayerful reflection sets in. The discerning sense that a less superficial view of restoration and reconstruction is called for. When restoration drags on, the wise come to realise that perhaps the 'return' was nowhere near radical enough. The community come to prayer again: 'Will you not revive us again [O God our Saviour], that your people may rejoice in you?' (v.6).

In four stanzas, we overhear their prayer and God's stunning answer to it (vv.1–3; 4–7; 8–9; 10–13).

Firstly, we hear *a heart-warming precedent* (vv.1–3)

'You showed favour once Lord … you forgave and restored in our past history – do it again, Lord.' Nostalgia need not breed inertia but can be a powerful incentive to seek God's favour again. Small children have a tireless ability of asking you to repeat a story or a playtime activity over and over again. 'Do it again ...', they say ad infinitum! They never seem to weary of repetition. And parents and grown-ups do it again until they drop. But perhaps, as G.K. Chesterton observed, where adults fail,

> God is strong enough to exult in monotony. It is possible that God says every morning, 'Do it again' to the sun; and every evening 'Do it again' to the moon ... It may be that God has the eternal appetite of infancy; for we have sinned and grown old, and our Father is younger than we are.[95]

Perhaps now is the time to stop being resigned to the way things are; perhaps it's the moment to overcome embarrassment and embrace a 'second naiveté' which is childlike enough to ask, 'Do it again, Lord.'

What follows is a *heartfelt prayer* (vv.4-7)

God Himself is our only hope and greatest need. A half-renewed, half-restored Church needs God more not less. The contemporary charismatic Church especially has exhausted all the branded options and been wearied in the welldoing of them. In the end when we've 'discipled' it, 'apostled' it, 'named and claimed' it, amplified it, 'Wimber-ised' it, 'Peretti-ed' it, territorialised it, inner-healed it, 'Toronto-ed' it, counselled it, Spring Harvest-ed it, marched round it ... then with relief we turn to God again!

'The inevitable and constant preliminary to revival has always been a thirst for God, a thirst, a living thirst, for knowledge of the living God, and a longing and a burning desire to see him acting, manifesting himself and his power, rising, and scattering his enemies.'[96]

There is a paradox here. Initially we must recognise God as our greatest problem! Our most pressing anxiety is His anger and His displeasure (vv.3–5). The One Creator God revealed in the Bible is not the Immutable Force or Unmoved Mover of philosophical speculation. The God of the psalmist is 'bursting with pathos'.[97]

God takes Himself seriously, not out of vanity, but out of deep integrity and moral resolve; for this reason He takes us seriously, and probes our integrity and moral fidelity. He is no ironic post-modern deity, flip and arch, teasing us and putting us down with a throw-away line. He is straight and true, just and faithful and not about to compromise His own holiness with a pinch of salt. Only as we face God as our greatest problem can He become our salvation again. Without reckoning with His divine wrath there is no redemption, restoration or revival.

Thankfully, wrath is not second nature to Him but a reaction to our sin. Thankfully, without presuming on it, we can believe that 'his anger lasts only a moment, but his favour lasts a lifetime' (Psa. 30:5). So it is with our Saviour we plead (Psa. 85:4). He revives and restores. When He does, our joy is as unconfined as His love is unfailing (vv.6–7). Salvation is His greatest gift (v.7). We can ask for nothing more.

At this point in the interchange, a priest or prophet interrupts to give a *heart-stirring prophecy* (vv.8–9)

How quickly God can respond to truly desperate praying. Are we in a position to hear the answering prophetic voice as the psalmist was? Usually it is in the desert that the comforting voice is calling. Far from the madding crowd of the evangelical 'show-biz' world, in some obscure place, a lonely listener to God receives the reviving Word and renewing Spirit of God.

Visit the village of Llangeitho, in West Wales where the Great Awakening began in the eighteenth century through the ministry of Daniel Rowland. To this day it remains a quiet backwater, an out-of-the-way, unpretentious place. Just the sort of homely stage that the God bent on revival seems to prefer. And it's usually a sleepy matinee, deliberately to wrong foot the media crowd.

The prophet 'listens to what God the LORD will say' (v.8).

And as Tozer said, it pays to listen to the man who listens to God. It is always good news. Even God's judgments are good news since now we know with relief that there is someone who will tell us the truth about ourselves and can do something to rectify what's wrong.

God promises 'peace' to His people (v.8), 'peace' – 'shalom' – that all the biblical words perhaps best sums up the final vision of the Bible for a community living in tune with God in joy, well-being, harmony and prosperity.[98] In short, all that verses 10–13 envisage.

But there are at least three ground rules:

1. *No reviving without repentance (v.8d)*

God promises fresh disclosures of His grace and power but only as we repudiate our foolish ways, have done with casual Christianity and commit ourselves to the wild adventure again.

2. *No nearness without 'fearness' (v.9)*

The fresh bracing air of the 'fear of the LORD' must be let into the stuffy, sleep-inducing 'fug' of over-heated religiosity. Let the tame gods die and the wild God reappear. Stop trying to domesticate the Tiger and give back His majesty and freedom. By trite songs, trivial prophecies, cheap grace and cost-free evangelism, we have tried to make God 'user-friendly'. But a 'user-friendly' God is a false God. The real God is awesome in close-up.

3. *No salvation without glory (v.9)*

And the glory is for Him!

We best respond to the promise of revival by determining from the outset not to take the credit. The God who shares His glory with 'no other' is set on exalting His name not on providing publicity for high-profile Christian leaders. Will we never learn? Trust not the popular propagandists of revival – already cashing in with their best-selling paperbacks on their small corner of the revival. Trust not those who are already using the merest hint of revival to enhance their celebrity status in the Christian media. Trust the aged pioneers and lonely widows who have borne the burden of interceding for whatever way God chooses to glory Himself. Beyond every felt need of ours lies an absolute necessity of His, that 'His glory may dwell in our land'.

The prophet offers heart-stopping prospects. The psalmist is offered the fascinating prospect of a reunion of the divine attributes! Here are the trademark qualities of a covenant-keeping God: steadfast-love ('*hesed*'), faithfulness, righteousness and peace. No regimental or college reunion was ever like this. Love and faithfulness are reunited. The days of cheap grace (of grace without discipleship) are over. The days of sentimental love (of love without commitment) are gone. Love meets up with covenant again and become inseparable. Righteousness comes down from heaven and faithfulness rises up to embrace it. This coalition of holiness is more than a match for any axis of evil. Love and faithfulness, justice and peace – these allies invade the land and God's glory dwells in it.

What follows is an amazing reconciliation of all that has been torn asunder by sin:

- *Heaven and earth agree* (v.11) – the spiritual no longer divorced from the material, the sacred at one with the secular because all is 'holy' to the Lord.

- *The Lord and the land are reconciled* (v.12) – faith no longer split off from politics, the Church no longer a pietistic ghetto, the supernatural displayed in the supermarket, the whole land flooded with glory.

- *Leader and led now walk in step together* (v.13) – the credibility gap closed between believing and behaving, our joy complete as we cross new frontiers in keeping pace with righteousness.

This is a glimpse of new creation, a world of 'full harmonization'.[99]

This is 'the neighbourly engagement of ground and sky, heaven and earth, God and people'.[100]

This sounds like revival. 'Do it Lord, do it again.'

Prayer and Reflections

Lord, I am hurting
Praying the psalms encourages me to release to You my cry
  of pain.
I feel battered, depressed, confused.
Absorb my angry questions and answer me with reassurance
  of Your love.

As for my sin, Lord, I find it easier to make general confession
  of my guilt than to own up to specific sins.
But I name my sins for what they are, insults to Your grace.
I have betrayed trust and have often offended against love.
I don't like to think of myself as unreliable but I am.
I do withdraw from You and from those close to me, hugging
  my pride or self-pity to myself.
Forgive my sins according to Your mercy. I plead the blood
  of Jesus Christ to cleanse me from all unrighteousness.
Fill me with your Holy Spirit today Lord, to create in me
  a clean heart and renew a right spirit in me.

Lord, it is sometimes grievous to consider the condition
  of Your people.
Send revival.
Do it again Lord. Do it in Your way and in Your time.
Send Your Spirit sweeping through Your Church that Your
  glory may again dwell in our land.
For Your name's sake,
Amen.

- Right now, pour out to the Lord all and every feeling you have
  – however negative. Surrender to Him your disappointments,
  your anger, and any unresolved issues. Hand over to Him your
  unanswered questions.

He has a great shock-absorbing heart.

- Confess your sins to a trusted friend, minister, pastor or priest, together finding assurance of God's forgiveness.

- Revisit the most desperate times in your life and recall how the Lord ministered to you and brought you through.

- With a Christian friend, your spouse, or members of your house-group compose a lament for the Church. Discuss how well this would fit into your normal style of worship. Pray today for revival.

- Discuss with others the difference between a 'wintry spirituality' and a 'summery spirituality'. Is this merely a matter of temperament? How can each enrich the other and live together in peace?

SPRING SONGS

PSALMS

'... hope springs eternal ...'

All praise is prophetic activity. This is not so much in directly predicting the future but in making us more immediately aware of God.

As we have said, in the praise of God in the Psalms we are 'at full stretch before God'. It is not surprising that we are drawn out of ourselves by such an experience. The beauty of God attracts us and kindles desire in us. The prospect of God gives new direction to our lives, new impetus and motivation. God's future quickens our imagination to project new scenarios of God's arrivals and renewals.

This is to embark on what A.W. Tozer called, 'the heart's happy exploration of the infinite riches of the Godhead'.[101]

In the praise of God we reach out to respond to the Lord we know who is yet waiting to be known.

In praise we reach out to the God among us who is yet over us and beyond us.

In praise we reach out to the God with us who is yet ahead of us.

In the words of Daniel Hardy and David Ford,

> to rejoice in this God is a prophetic act which at once stings the habitual worldly wisdom fed on suspicion, bad news, and equivocal of cynical judgments. It also stings the practical atheism of many 'believers'. Actually to carry through in practice belief in a good God to the extreme of making his goodness the spring of continued thanks and praise; that is to take God seriously and therefore too joyfully.[102]

Divine discontent works on three levels:

(a) *Personally*, God becomes the goal of our striving, the end of our searching, the food and drink we crave, the satisfaction of our soul.

(b) *Corporately*, we seek to go up to the festival, to be the community of the King where we covet the times and places in which His gracious goodness binds us together, and love unites us (eg Psa.133).

(c) *Politically*, our hopes are aroused of the coming of God's ideal king and kingship and fills the horizon of our vision and dreams. By declaring the majesty of God and proclaiming the fullness of His grace, prophetic praise changes the way we do our politics.

So these psalms, which I have somewhat arbitrarily grouped together, nevertheless have much in common. They herald God as the most worthy of honour and the most attractive goal to be sought, and in doing so arouse hunger and thirst for new knowledge of God. They serve to galvanise discipleship in moving in the direction of God, stimulating our desire to seek and know God better and to walk in His ways of worship and obedience together. They celebrate God as the supreme prize to be won, and turn us towards Zion and to the community of the King.

Deep longing for God Himself in turn fuels desire for God's dwelling place in Zion, directs our feet in the highways to Zion and stirs us to active discipleship and obedience; this in turn generates heartfelt passion for God's kingdom and ideal King to come!

Negative experiences can be positive incentives to reach out to God again. Emptiness, due to the failure of alternative and now broken cisterns, drives us to the fountain again. Dissatisfaction about where we are and the company we keep (Psa. 121) drives us to heed the call to pilgrimage and spurs us to go up to the feast together. The demise of kingship in Israel concentrated devout minds wonderfully. It brought into sharp focus the need to seek first God's kingdom and the King who embodies it.

Let's consider further the three dimensions of hope:

- aspiration
- ascent
- anticipation

(a) aspiration – pursuit of God

If we are to seek after God as the supreme prize, we must believe that God is good and that He is out for our best interests. To seek God's glory as our greatest good is to be convinced that our happiness and His holiness coincide. It is to dare to believe that through redemption the pathways of pleasure and the paths of righteousness can once more converge. John Piper has championed this fervently in recent years. He has staked his whole ministry on the fact that 'God is most glorified in us when we are most satisfied in him.'[103] As he puts it in another place, 'God's pursuit of praise from us and our pursuit of pleasure in him are the same pursuit'.[104]

This is the joy of what he calls 'Christian hedonism'. Its roots are in the psalmists' consistent longing after God. 'In the end, the heart longs not for any of God's good gifts but for God himself. To see him and know him and be in his presence is the soul's final feast. Beyond this there is no quest. Words fail. We call it pleasure, joy, delight. But these are weak pointers to the unspeakable experience.'[105] Such is the power of love that the heart desires. 'The Christian hedonist pursues love because he is addicted to the experience of that power. He wants to feel more and more of the grace of God reigning in his life.'[106]

It is surely significant that in all the prayer reports recorded in his letters, the apostle Paul prays essentially for one thing for the churches in his care: that they might know God better.

Idolatry is the 'suicidal exchange of infinite value and beauty for some fleeting, inferior substitute'.[107] All sin is sacrilege, the debasement of powers and potential implanted in us by God. Sin expresses our failure to value God supremely and our liability to expend disproportionate devotion on lesser objects, even legitimate ones. The wisdom here is to renounce sin but not to repudiate whatever is good in creation. Rather we should seek their legitimate satisfaction within God, His will and His ways, His energy and passion.

'Our desire, if we will listen to it, will save us from committing soul-suicide, the sacrifice of our hearts on the altar of "getting by".'[108]

(b) ascent – pilgrimage to Zion

I live barely five miles from the ancient Pilgrim's Way, the route taken by devout medieval marchers between the great cathedrals of Winchester and Canterbury. But such piety was alien to the evangelicalism in which I was raised. Despite the almost iconic status of Bunyan's *Pilgrim's Progress* in our tradition, the evangelicals of my youth were suspicious of ideas of pilgrimage. There were at least two reasons for this, I believe. On the one hand we associated such concepts with Catholics and for us they were therefore off-limits. Journeying to Compestala or Lourdes seemed dangerously pre-Reformation notions. At the same time we deemed such concepts to have a vaguely liberal tinge to them, hinting at uncertainty about our security and salvation. Pilgrimage we feared detracted from the 'past tense' of salvation. The doctrines of justification by faith and assurance seemed threatened by talk of journeys and discovery.

Something precious was no doubt being defended here – the absolute fact that here and now we can embrace the 'joyful news of sins forgiven and peace with heaven' and that, here and now, we have been transferred from the kingdom of darkness to the kingdom of God's Beloved Son. But much was lost, too, by our fear.

Evangelicalism has perhaps unwittingly given the impression that salvation is a matter of accepting the five things you must believe as a package deal for salvation, with the result that we now have our ticket to heaven in our pocket – and no doubt God too – and that all that remains is to get on with the practical job of doing God's will.

Against this attitude the songs of ascent guard us. They inspire us to keep seeking, to keep moving on. In ancient Israel all men were expected to make the trip to Jerusalem three times a year for the major feasts. It is an interesting irony to note that now every self-respecting evangelical Christian embarks on a pilgrimage of one sort or another, even if only to the Holy Land. Evangelicals will now also be found on Lindisfarne, in guided retreats around Holy Island. Every year, too, in the UK, thousands of evangelicals relish the prospect of 'going up to the festival' by gathering at New Wine or Spring Harvest or Stoneleigh or wherever the current 'high spot' of the year is located.

At the deeper level of theological significance, a case can be made for the whole Bible being a story of pilgrimage. Launched by Abraham's obedience to God's call to leave and go, the journey was not terminated by the promised land but remains the pathway to be trodden by God's people as they walk in the footsteps of Father Abraham (Rom. 4). The journey which began then eventually leads from the city of man to the city of God (Heb. 11). In this sense we are – as the first Christians were called – still 'followers of the Way'.

The songs of ascent instruct us that this journey is best made prayerfully and joyfully and in conscious solidarity with our fellow pilgrims.

(c) anticipation – prophetic yearning for the advent of God's King and kingdom

In understanding the Old Testament, it would be difficult to overestimate the importance of kingship.

As we have noted, Psalms 2–72 offer a positive view of Davidic kingship and include those songs associated with him. This is modified in Psalms 73–88 in response to the Exilic experience. A once favourable view of kingship is then re-evaluated in Psalm 89 in the light of the tragic history of royal failure. The haunting question hangs in the air: does God's covenant with David still hold?

Psalms 90–106 provide an editorial answer to Psalm 89 by reaffirming the faith of the pre-monarchical Mosaic period. Significantly, Psalm 90 is deemed to be a song of Moses. Now, after the Exile, as it was in Mosaic times, Yahweh alone and unequivocally is King. He can be trusted now, even after human monarchy has disappeared.

So Psalm 93 echoes perhaps the coronation of the King with its reaffirmation of Yahweh's kingship in an annual festival which may have been attached to the Tabernacles Feast.

In Psalm 95 we are urged to listen to the King's Word when in the King's presence. A prophet speaker warns (v.7ff) that exuberant worship can mask hardness of heart to what God is wanting to say, so effectively crowding Him out.

There is a movement in these psalms from God's present rule, through His coming in the future to judge and save (Psa. 96, 98) and then to His reigning again (Psa. 97, 99). We can capture this flow of thought by setting the two pairs of psalms alongside each other.

Psalms 96-97	98-99
Sing a new song 96:1	Sing a new song 98:1
Summon earth to praise Him 96:7ff	Earth to rejoice 98:4–6
The reigning Lord comes 96:13	The Lord comes 98:9
Result: The Lord reigns 97:1	The Lord reigns 99:1
Worship the exalted Lord 97:6ff	Exalt the exalted Lord 99:5
Praise His holy name 97:12	For the Lord is holy 99:9

The 'new song' encapsulates the good news that the 'Lord who is King', who even now 'reigns' is also the King who is 'coming' to implement and establish His rule in a final way.

The repeated 'trisagion' in Psalm 99 'Holy ... holy ... holy ...' is significant. This antiphonal cry was associated previously with the ark of the covenant. But though this item of sacred furniture was lacking in the post-Exilic Temple (see Jer. 3), it is still sung in heaven's worship (see Isa. 6). This is to remind us that worship is not something we initiate but something already and always going on in which we participate!

Psalm 132 too is an old ark song (see 1 Chron. 13–16; 2 Sam. 5–6) once sung at the dedication of the Temple, now sung by pilgrims on the way to feast. How does this work? Note that the second half of the psalm matches the aspirations of the first. Verses 1–10 are prayers based on promises made to David (2 Sam. 7). Verses 11–18 are a prophecy affirming the promises made to the king.

(A) Four prayers vv.1–10:	(B) God's fourfold answer
(i) remember oath to David vv.1–5	(i) 'I will set ...' v.11
(ii) arise to your resting-place vv.6–8	(ii) 'This is ... I will ...' v.13f
(iii) may your priests ... v.9	(iii) 'I will clothe ...' v.16
(iv) don't abandon your anointed servant David v.10	(iv) 'I will honour David's line ...' vv.17–18

In other words, God's answers perfectly match the aspirations of the Davidic kingship in Israel.

Yet by its placement in what we have seen is essentially a post-Davidic section of the Psalms, something more seems to be implied than a straightforward re-endorsement of the Davidic kingship as we have known it so far. Set where it is on the other side of the post-monarchical watershed marked by Psalm 89, Psalm 132 strongly suggests that God will keep His royal promises. God will fulfil all the potential inherent in the office of king. But He will do this on His own terms in His own time. He will not do so by restoring the status quo, by reinstating the former kind of Davidic kingship that has so evidently failed.

Rather, He will bring in a new kind of 'Davidic' king through whom to achieve His royal plans. Delegated kingship passes back into His hands to be reminted as true Sonship. In this way messianic dreams are reignited. The rivers of praise which celebrate human kingship in Israel will one day overspill their banks and flood the Church with images of Jesus. So we find hymns in praise of Jesus Christ within the New Testament itself (Col. 1:15–20; Phil. 2:5–11; 1 Tim. 3:16). Fascinatingly, these are the highest points of the apostolic understanding of Jesus in the whole New Testament and were very likely produced in context of Spirit-inspired worship.

New Testament theologian, Ben Witherington, comments on this remarkable feature. 'Though perhaps it is an exaggeration to say that early Christology was born in song, one may certainly say that early Christology grew out of the worship of Christ ...'[109]

Martin Hengel, the German New Testament scholar, wrote the seminal article on this in 1980.[110] In his view, 'the hymn to Christ served as a living medium for the progressive development of christological thinking'. This happened most likely in worship where 'through its Risen and Exalted Lord the community stood in a direct connection with the heavenly sanctuary and through the Spirit the Lord himself was present in it'. We may surmise that this involved the use of psalms like Psalms 2, 45, 72, and 110 and interpreted messianically. Celebrating Christ's victory and moved by the sense of His presence with them, the worshippers sang through and beyond these ancient texts to new expressions of praise to Jesus. 'The Spirit,' Hengel suggests, 'urged them on beyond the content of preaching, the exegesis of scripture and indeed the content of confessional formulae expressed in prose to express new, bolder, greater things in the "new song" of the hymn to Christ, because earthbound human language could not do justice to God."[111]

Aspiration, ascent, anticipation

There is, then, a keen prophetic edge to biblical praise and worship. The pursuit of God for each soul's satisfaction, the pilgrimage to our destiny together in God, the prophetic vision of the kingdom for the world – in military terms they extend the supply-lines of faith to dangerously vulnerable frontiers.

These are the keynotes of praise 'at full stretch before God'. In Ellen Davis's words, 'People who pray are people living in hope. From a biblical perspective, hope may best be imaged as a line suspended between past experience of God's reliability and a future that is still open, stretched taut between the reliability and the freedom of Israel's God.'[112]

Worship is above all the context in which

... a man's reach should exceed his grasp,
Or what's a heaven for? (Browning)

Praise takes us beyond previous boundaries. In Brueggemann's words:

Praise is a glad statement of 'disbelief', an acknowledgement that there is more to the reality of Yahweh than we dared to hope and more than we could have imagined. Doxology is an irrational act that pushes beyond control, summons us beyond our cherished rationality, rescues us from anxiety, transcends despair, overrides arrogance, strips us of self-sufficiency, and leaves us unreservedly and entirely entrusted to this Other One who cares for us more than we care for ourselves.[113]

ASPIRATION

Deep Calls to Deep (Psalms 42-43)

Psalm 42
For the director of music. A *maskil* of the Sons of Korah.

[1]As the deer pants for streams of water,
 so my soul pants for you, O God.
[2]My soul thirsts for God, for the living God.
 When can I go and meet with God?
[3]My tears have been my food
 day and night,
while men say to me all day long,
 'Where is your God?'
[4]These things I remember
 as I pour out my soul:
how I used to go with the multitude,
 leading the procession to the house of God,
with shouts of joy and thanksgiving
 among the festive throng.

[5]Why are you downcast, O my soul?
 Why so disturbed within me?
Put your hope in God,
 for I will yet praise him,
 my Saviour and [6]my God.

My soul is downcast within me;
   therefore I will remember you
from the land of the Jordan,
   the heights of Hermon – from Mount Mizar.
⁷Deep calls to deep
   in the roar of your waterfalls;
all your waves and breakers
   have swept over me.

⁸By day the LORD directs his love,
   at night his song is with me –
a prayer to the God of my life.

⁹I say to God my Rock,
   'Why have you forgotten me?
Why must I go about mourning,
   oppressed by the enemy?'
¹⁰My bones suffer mortal agony
   as my foes taunt me,
saying to me all day long,
   'Where is your God?'

¹¹Why are you downcast, O my soul?
   Why so disturbed within me?
Put your hope in God,
   for I will yet praise him,
   my Saviour and my God.

Psalm 43
¹Vindicate me, O God,
   and plead my cause against an ungodly nation;
   rescue me from deceitful and wicked men.
²You are God my stronghold.
   Why have you rejected me?

Why must I go about mourning,
    oppressed by the enemy?
³Send forth your light and your truth,
    let them guide me;
let them bring me to your holy mountain,
    to the place where you dwell.
⁴Then will I go to the altar of God,
    to God, my joy and my delight.
I will praise you with the harp,
    O God, my God.

⁵Why are you downcast, O my soul?
    Why so disturbed within me?
Put your hope in God,
    for I will yet praise him,
    my Saviour and my God.

LISTENING IN TO THESE PSALMS IS A BIT LIKE BEING A
guest in an operating theatre where open-heart surgery is going
on. What we're looking at here is 'open-soul surgery'!

I find the psalmist's frankness refreshing. Unlike so many
prayers, here is no cover-up job. We are adept at concocting
prayers that sound dependent but make us appear self-sufficient.
Fluency in prayer can make us sound more spiritually healthy
than we really are. My false self, the great imposter, disguises itself
as a smiling believer in the hope that I can make it undetected
through another song, or time of worship. This pattern of
camouflage continues the elaborate game we were taught in
childhood: play your part well, don't let reality spoil a good pose,
don't laugh or cry, and speak when you're spoken to! So in worship
we face the front and look interested but our eyes give us away,
lacking spark and engagement, and, behind the mask, our minds
whirl away at our own agendas. With their searing honesty, the
Psalms blow our cover.

So here the psalmist offers no religious PR talk, designed to fob God off with bland religious talk and put him in a good light. He says what he feels – that God has forgotten him (42:9). Not for the psalmist: 'I'm sure You were thinking of me on my birthday but being such an important person You were far too busy to send a card. I quite understand.'

NO: 'You forgot, didn't You?' (v.9).

This is not even 'damning God with faint praise'!

So the brutal honesty of psalms like this is disconcerting but is at the same time a wonderful encouragement to us to get real with God. The psalmist peels off the layers of his soul to leave his heart exposed and to reveal his deepest longings (42:1–3). He lays bare how deeply despairing and disturbed he is in his soul (42:5, 11; see also 43:5).

Two factors appear to have contributed to his state of mind. Firstly, he is evidently cut off from the Temple and distanced from its worship through some kind of exile or even illness. Whatever the specific cause of his condition, it has left him disorientated and alone. Secondly, his downcast state of mind – which on the surface gives scant evidence of faith – leaves him open to the mockery of unbelievers who taunt him to show signs of God in his life. 'Where is your God?' is the jibe (42:3, 10; see 43:2).

This then is the lament of a parched and beleaguered man. He has nothing to lose and so bears his soul to God in prayer.

'Water' is the key imagery the psalmist employs.

- Living water evokes the depth of the soul's thirst for God, the source of life (42:1–2).
- Tears are the outpouring of the soul's despair at the absence of God (42:3–4, 9–10).
- Waterfalls and waves evoke the depths in God of mercy and judgment (42:5, 7, 11).

'Thirst' is the first metaphor used and it evokes the depths of longings in the human heart. The image of a doe stooping wearily to find water catches well the downcast bend of a parched soul.

Perhaps it starts with the psalmist's general dissatisfaction with life. It is as if nothing glows anymore; everything is dull; nothing leaps in one's life but only limps along. The psalmist is pressed to ask: Why?

Larry Crabb has analysed this dissatisfaction on three levels, as casual longings, critical longings and crucial longings.[114]

In my *casual longings* I want England to win, must have a coffee, must do the garden (very casual this one!), must buy a dog, take a vacation, and so on. Still the dissatisfaction lingers on.

My *critical longings* operate at a slightly deeper level. Every one of us wants to be loved and wanted; wants to feel that we matter, that we count for something in the great order of things. We fear being obliterated by the incoming tide of time like footprints on the sand. So we long for friendship, love and relationships, and the intimacy, security and acceptance we assume they will bring. In them we envisage our thirst being quenched. To that end we want to succeed at work, or want our children to succeed at school and so strive for self-fulfilment in careers and family. But the suspicion nags away …

Beneath all, in the depths of the soul, stir *crucial longings*. James L. Mays says it straight: 'The dissatisfaction of life is the thirst for God.' He comments, 'The body cannot live without water. Its lack, quicker than anything else except breath itself, is felt as desperate desire. The soul cannot survive without God. That is true of every human soul, not just the deeply pious. Many or most may not understand the thirst that disturbs and drives their living, but it is there because God created the human soul to correspond to God.'[115]

So candidly the psalmist opens his heart and begins to break through his despair. As he expresses his deepest feelings, special times and special places begin to reconnect him with faith and hope. We dare not try to be more spiritual than God. Ours is a creational and incarnational faith. Space and time are channels by which we receive God's life, not hindrances to it. Dates and faces, festivals and celebrations fix themselves in our memory as means of grace.

So with the psalmist. Memories of those special times of festival processions in Jerusalem and joyful entry to God's house come flooding back to pierce the gloom (42:4). And special places matter too. Any old bush will do for God's burning glory to show itself. In his 'exile' in the land of Jordan near the headwaters of the river at Mount Hermon, the psalmist looks around him (42:6–7). The spectacular scenery and dramatic natural phenomena reawaken his jaded senses and depressed spirit. From this 'sacred' spot, the psalmist remembers God.

Deep calls to deep

Standing there next to the crashing waterfalls and tumbling waves, the psalmist is given an audio-visual reminder of the powerful deep currents of God's judgment and love which have broken over him. The surging, roaring water may even have evoked the memory of the torrent of noisy worshippers pouring out of the sanctuary at festival time.

In this way 'deep calls to deep', the depths in God's own grace and justice experienced in worship answer to the deep longings of the human soul. So Psalm 42 faces the urgent need for God, the God who is my life. It does so with the strange and paradoxical recognition that the longing for God – like longing for a drink – is somehow part of the pleasure to be gained from finding Him!

We can be encouraged by the psalmist to grow wise in the following ways:

1. *Don't be fobbed off with anything less than God.*
Don't settle, as Duncan Campbell famously put it, 'for anything less than heaven wills to give us'.

In his famous children's book, *The Little Prince*, the pioneer French aviator and writer, Antoine de Saint-Exupéry, has the hero approached by a merchant selling pills that had been invented to quench thirst. Swallow one pill a week and you would feel no need of anything to drink.

"'Why are you selling those pills?" asked the little prince. "Because they save a tremendous amount of time," said the merchant. "Computations have been made by experts. With these pills, you save fifty-three minutes in every week."

"'And what would I do with those fifty-three minutes?"

"Anything you like ..."

"'As for me," said the little prince to himself, "if I had fifty-three minutes to spend as I like, I should walk at my leisure to a spring of fresh water.'"[116]

Be encouraged by the psalmist to:

2. Talk to yourself.
In spiritual matters this is a sign of health not madness. 'Why are you downcast, O my soul ...' (42:5, 11; 43:5). As that wise physician of souls as well as bodies, Dr Martyn Lloyd-Jones, shrewdly put it: 'We must talk to ourselves, instead of allowing "ourselves" to talk to us. Most of your unhappiness in life is due to the fact that you are listening to yourself instead of talking to yourself.'[117] In Abraham Heschel's words, 'A person is what he aspires to. In order to know myself, I ask: what are the ends I am striving to attain? What are the values I care for most? What are the great yearnings I should like to be moved by?'[118]

3. Recall past occasions when you felt the presence of God, perhaps with other people.
'Empty out the pockets of your life,' as Peterson puts it (*The Message*).

I remember my first pastor, John Tugwell, preaching like an angel on the Cross and Resurrection and casting a lasting Easter spell upon me. I remember, along with my fellow students, a Billy Graham rally in a bleak and windswept football stadium where we were far too cold to fall for any emotionalism and it could only have been God who provoked the response I saw with my own eyes.

I remember Fountain Trust meetings and Fisherfolk concerts when Holy Spirit heaven seemed in the air. I remember baptisms in my first pastoral charge in Kingfield, Woking and exuberant celebrations at Capel Bible Week. I remember the King's Church where like the psalmist 'I was at the head of the worshipping crowd ... leading them all, eager to arrive and worship' (*The Message*). I have a history with God and it isn't all bad!

Nostalgia can provoke reality. And listening to Mozart's *Exsultate Jubilate* sung by Elly Ameling, or Robin Mark in Belfast leading 1,000 men in singing 'Will your anchor hold in the storms of life?' or Gordon Fee on tape lecturing about virtually anything – and longings after God are re-aroused.

Even the waves of blackness and sorrow that have engulfed life are His waves (42:7). Even these have His signature on them. When fighting for life in a torrent of troubles that threatens to sweep me away, God is my rock in that raging river (42:9).

These reflections encourage the psalmist and us to take the big risk of trusting God again (42:5,11; 43:5)! 'Hope in God,' he tells himself, 'for I shall again praise him'. Risking all on God is – in a word – risky! Alienated as you feel from the centre of the action, haunted by the accusing voices that tell you that you are not offering much proof of God's being alive in your life, take the risk of trusting again!

From being at his lowest the psalmist is raised to his highest. 'Send forth your light and your truth, let them guide me; let them bring me to your holy mountain, to the place where you dwell' (Psa. 43:3).

Deep calls to deep; calls us out of the depths and up to the heights. Streams, tears, waterfalls, waves are sourced by the snows in the distant hills.

Thirsty in the Rain (Psalm 63)

A psalm of David. When he was in the Desert of Judah.

[1]O God, you are my God,
   earnestly I seek you;
my soul thirsts for you,
   my body longs for you,
in a dry and weary land
   where there is no water.

[2]I have seen you in the sanctuary
   and beheld your power and your glory.
[3]Because your love is better than life,
   my lips will glorify you.
[4]I will praise you as long as I live,
   and in your name I will lift up my hands.
[5]My soul will be satisfied as with the richest of foods;
   with singing lips my mouth will praise you.

[6]On my bed I remember you;
   I think of you through the watches of the night.
[7]Because you are my help,
   I sing in the shadow of your wings.
[8]My soul clings to you;
   your right hand upholds me.

[9]They who seek my life will be destroyed;
   they will go down to the depths of the earth.
[10]They will be given over to the sword
   and become food for jackals.

[11]But the king will rejoice in God;
   all who swear by God's name will praise him,

while the mouths of liars will be silenced.

RELIGION IS NOW LISTED ON SOME INTERNET CATEGORIES among 'leisure pursuits'; not a new development though. There have always been people with a religious bent for whom religion is a well-preserved hobby, a spare-time activity on a par with hang-gliding or stamp collecting.

What is odd is that the Church should have contributed to this state of affairs by its perennial tendency to fudge the main reason for its existence.

Join the Scottish expatriate association and you might expect to spend most of your time extolling the virtues of Scotland. A Scotsman I knew once often disappeared from college to enjoy an evening of Highland dancing led by kilted pipers or to watch films of the Trossachs, Cairngorms or the Edinburgh Military Tattoo!

Move in with the philatelic crowd and you can be sure to become a stamp-nut; fall in with the hang-gliders and expect to run over the side of a few mountains. And as for full-time occupations, how many people virtually eat, sleep and drink politics or business or sport?

So what might we expect a community of believers to be pre-occupied with? You might assume it would be so taken up with God as to be God-obsessed. Sadly, looking at the modern Church, you might be wrong. In which case we need to feel the thrust of psalms like this one. For these old songs of Israel are disconcertingly God-centred, are they not? Make no mistake about it, these ancient troubadours of faith were obsessed with God. If we watch them, they may help us sharpen our blurred vision of what we are about. Listening to their songs could well revive our jaded appetite for the one real reason for our existence, which is God Himself!

A.W. Tozer was one of those pioneering souls who sought to renew the knowledge of God in the modern Church. He longed, he said, for a Church where God was the only explanation and God was the only attraction. He wrote of his own generation:

There are increasing numbers of persons whose lives are marked by a growing hunger after God himself. They are athirst for God. They will not be satisfied until they have drunk deep at the Fountain of Living Water. This is the only real harbinger of revival which I have been able to detect anywhere on the religious horizon.[119]

In Psalm 63 the singer invites us to renew our obsession with God by sampling his own: 'O God, you are my God, earnestly I seek you' (v.1).

The Greek philosopher, Pythagoras, is reputed to have said that there are three kinds of seeker:

- *The seeker after knowledge* whose modern intellectual counterparts remain indebted to Greek influence on education and learning.
- *The seeker after fame*, well matched in our world by the celebrities who are famous for being famous in a star-struck media culture.
- *The seeker after gain*, materialist to the bone, for whom everything in life is a commodity.

But the sage omitted the 'seeker after God'.

The wise man in Israel was in no doubt as to God's view of our priorities, 'I love those who love me, and those who seek me find me' (Prov. 8:17). The prophet confirms it: 'My soul yearns for you in the night; in the morning my spirit longs for you' (Isa. 26:9).

Seeker-friendly services became fashionable during the 1990s in churches within the Western World. All well and good, providing that it was not only superficial felt-needs that were being met but the real deeper need of the human heart for the life of God itself.

The psalmist's concentration here is fierce: his soul thirsts for God (v.1). His bodily constitution faint with hunger, his enervated condition, dehydration and exhaustion vividly symbolise his consuming desire for God.

The psychiatrist, Richard Winter, has brilliantly explored how boredom characterises contemporary society. Where there are no restraints, the borders of what is permissible are pushed further and further back. People easily tire of one sensation and press for a greater adrenaline rush. This may push them into extreme sports like bungee jumping or it may drive them to drugs or violent crime. An over-satiated society faces slow death by boredom. Mary Pipher points out the ironies which abound in the modern world: 'With more entertainment, we are bored. With more sexual information and stimulation, we experience less sexual pleasure. In a culture focused on feelings, people grow emotionally numb. We are (to quote Peter Rowan) "thirsty in the rain".'[120]

Soaked through with post-modern irony and flip punch lines, drenched by a downpour of non-stop electronic diversion, showered endlessly with advertising and hype, saturated with entertainment, we nevertheless remain 'thirsty in the rain'. Richard Winter himself pleads for a recovery of passion and wonder in God: 'We are to be people of deep feeling and passion, aware that outer feelings need to be redeemed from their distortion and deadness and given full rein in the service of their Maker.'[121]

His soul feasts on God (v.5)
And is satisfied. Imagine your favourite meal, washed down with fine wine, a sumptuous feast, a celebration dinner or a square meal set before you when you come home ravenously hungry – this, says the psalmist, pictures his satisfaction in God!

The Bible often pictures the gospel as an invitation to a party, to an almighty 'bash' of sumptuous proportions and lip-smacking expectancy. God 'spreads a table before me', offers wine and milk with money and without price and in His Son, Jesus, calls us to the kingdom feast.

That querky Episcopalian, Robert Farrer Capon characterised the Reformation as:

a time when men went blind, staggering drunk because they discovered in the dusty basement of late medievalism, a whole cellarful of fifteen-hundred-year-old, two hundred proof grace – of bottle after bottle of pure distillate of Scripture, one sip of which would convince anyone that God saves us single-handedly.[122]

His soul clings to God (v.8)

This is bold language used of love, marriage and covenanted friendship. The psalmist 'cleaves' as Ruth did, when she would not let Naomi or God go! The psalmist hangs on to the God who is hanging on to him! Like one reaching down to a man who has slipped on to a precarious ledge and holding him, preventing him from falling, so the faller is held but only as he himself grips as tightly as he can!

The Bible college where I was first trained for the ministry was founded by the famous Victorian preacher, C.H. Spurgeon. Its motto was Spurgeon's own and showed a hand gripping a cross with the Latin tag: *'et teneo et teneor'* – 'I hold and am held'.

For the soul that is satisfied in God, feasts on Him and holds fast to Him, the result is joy, sheer joy. 'My lips will glorify you' (v.3), 'I will praise you as long as I live' (v.4), 'I will lift up my hands' (v.4b), 'with singing lips my mouth will praise you' (v.5).

Now, the big question is: How on earth did the psalmist let this God-obsession happen? How did he come to be in this state? After all, religion is artfully designed to keep God in His place! And His place is usually a safe distance from us in what Hans Urs von Balthasar once called 'God's game reserve, the national park of his churches'. There God is allowed quietly to graze without disturbance and without interference from Monday to Friday. Then at weekends the curious take a drive to see if God's still there and even to admire how well He is looking! So we treat Him as a comforting backdrop to life, the background music while business goes on as usual. He may be dutifully acknowledged, prayed to and even believed in, but He is essentially a sideshow.

But psalms like this post a warning notice in front of us. Be careful not to let this God get too close. He is a fire that wants to set you on fire. As von Hugel said, He wants to put salt in your mouth that you might thirst for Him more. This God desires nearness. He seeks trust and intimacy. He is a beggar for your love. He casts a whirlwind of desire.

He may leap out and ambush you; He is a tiger outside His cage.

And somewhere, somehow, the psalmist fell for it. He let his mental, moral, aesthetic and spiritual defences down and let God in. God has got beneath his skin. 'Jesus has got into your blood, hasn't he?' said a Hindu to E. Stanley Jones: 'Yes, and he's raised my temperature,' the man with a mission replied.

It is God who is to blame for the psalmist's condition.

Didn't the psalmist know that God was this dangerous?

(a) *The psalmist is captivated by the overwhelming attractiveness of God!*
Notice the language: 'seek ... thirsts ... longs ... faints ... clings ... satisfied ...'

This is the language of intoxication, obsession, passion.

And God is responsible for this.

'You would not have sought me except I had first found you' (Pascal).

Or as the hymnwriter, F.W. Faber put it:

O for freedom, for freedom in worshipping God,
For the mountain top feeling of generous souls,
For the health, for the air, of the hearts deep and broad,
Where grace not in rills but in cataracts rolls!

Most good is the brisk wholesome service of fear,
And the calm wise obedience of conscience is sweet;
And good are all worships, all loyalties dear,
All promptitudes fitting, all services meet.

But none honours God like the thirst of desire ... And as Faber added,

And they who love God cannot love him by measure,
For their love is but hunger to love still better.

(b) *The psalmist is dazzled by an overpowering vision of God's power and glory (v.2)*
'I have ... beheld your power and your glory.'

As is well known, the Hebrew word for 'glory', '*kabod*' implies something that is heavy, weighty, and substantial. We can appreciate the force of this by contrasting this verse with one in the previous psalm. 'Lowborn men are but a breath, the highborn are but a lie; if weighed on a balance, they are nothing' (Psa. 62:9). The obvious implication here is not to trust in men but God. His trustworthiness compared to men's when weighed in a balance comes down heavily in favour of God (62:8,10).

David Wells has spoken perceptively of 'the weightlessness of God' in the modern world. Many still say in opinion polls they 'believe in God', he notes, but He is a 'weightless' God. That is, God does not impinge upon their lives, does not weigh with them in living life, makes no substantial difference to the way they think and behave. In practice, believing in such a God is very little different from not believing in Him![123]

Psalms like this celebrate a God of power and glory whose beauty is more radiant than His wonderful creation, whose interests are more commanding than ours, whose joy is more enriching than entertainment, whose judgments are more awe-inspiring than the evening news and whose truth is more compelling than 'the advertisers sweet fog of flattery and lies'.[124]

Such glory Abraham glimpsed, and for it left Ur (Acts 7:2–3).

This glory Moses longed to see but was denied until the Mount of Transfiguration (Exod. 33). It was just this glory that Paul believed he gazed on in the face of Jesus Christ (2 Cor. 4:6). No wonder he relished 'the solid joy and lasting treasure none but Zion's children know' of inheriting an 'eternal weight of glory'.

(c) *The psalmist is gripped by the over-riding love of God (v.3)*
He makes the astonishing claim that God's '*hesed*' is 'better than life'. Only fools and martyrs say this. Once again we meet this great covenant word: steadfast love, or covenant-love, love with built-in faithfulness. The psalmist sings: 'You are my God' (v.1) not because he has a pocket-sized deity in his possession, but because he has been loved by the One Creator God into a personal relationship.

To know such love from God is 'better than life'. Is this hyperbole? Can we take the psalmist seriously here? Knowing God and abiding in His love outweighs the need to hang on to our natural-born life as if it were all we had. The psalmist is a daring prophet. Not till Easter will we know for sure that many waters cannot quench love, and that love will not let us go, even in the valley of the shadow. Love which is 'better than life' is the trailer for 'to me, to live is Christ and to die is gain' (Phil. 1:21). Paul discovered that God proved His covenant-love to us because even when we were sinners hostile to Him, Christ, God's Son, died for us. Compared to this quality of life in love, death was of small account. Love which is 'better than life' anticipates the relativising of all that Paul had once held dear in his Jewish heritage – the special status as God's elect and special pride as a law-keeping zealot for God's righteousness. Compared to knowing the depth of God's covenant-love in Christ, all this counts for nothing.

Such love is better than the best life can offer. Compared to the quality of life in love, even death is of small account. Covenant love is better than life because of the indestructible seed of resurrection in it. Truly the psalmist sang more than he knew, though not more than he felt.

The concluding stanza starkly reminds us that the psalmist was no monastic mystic, in tune with the Infinite but out of touch with the harsh realities of the finite world of everyday. Far from it. His thirst for God has occupied him even at a time when he is beset by threats to his life (vv.9–10).

All of which only serves to highlight the tension between God's friends and His enemies. His enemies eventually get what they deserve: their deserts. His friends never get what they deserve, but rather what they don't deserve, which is grace (v.11). Those who seek the psalmist's life will be destroyed: those who seek the psalmist's God will find life.

> For the lack of desire is the ill of all ills,
> Many thousands through it the dark pathway have trod
> The balsam, the wine of predestinate wills
> Is a jubilant pining and longing for God.
>
> God loves to be longed for, He loves to be sought
> For he sought us himself with such longing and love
> He died for desire of us, marvelous thought
> And he yearns for us now to be with him above.[125]

'To have found God and still to pursue him is the soul's paradox of love', scorned by the irreligious and the religious alike, but 'justified in happy experience by the children of the burning heart.'[126]

'Nothing keeps God at the center of worship like the biblical conviction that the essence of worship is deep, heartfelt satisfaction in him, and the trembling pursuit of that satisfaction is why we are together.'[127]

Miss that and you will go 'thirsty even in the rain'.
Find it and we may together go 'singing in the rain'!

ASCENT

Highways in the Heart (Psalm 84)

For the director of music. According to *gittith*. Of the Sons of Korah.
A psalm.

¹How lovely is your dwelling-place,
  O LORD Almighty!
²My soul yearns, even faints,
  for the courts of the LORD;
my heart and my flesh cry out
  for the living God.

³Even the sparrow has found a home,
  and the swallow a nest for herself,
  where she may have her young –
a place near your altar,
  O LORD Almighty, my King and my God.
⁴Blessed are those who dwell in your house;
  they are ever praising you.   *Selah*

⁵Blessed are those whose strength is in you,
  who have set their hearts on pilgrimage.
⁶As they pass through the Valley of Baca,
  they make it a place of springs;
  the autumn rains also cover it with pools.
⁷They go from strength to strength,
  till each appears before God in Zion.
⁸Hear my prayer, O LORD God Almighty;
  listen to me, O God of Jacob.   *Selah*
⁹Look upon our shield, O God;
  look with favour on your anointed one.

[10]Better is one day in your courts
  than a thousand elsewhere;
I would rather be a doorkeeper in the house of my God
  than dwell in the tents of the wicked.
[11]For the LORD God is a sun and shield;
  the LORD bestows favour and honour;
no good thing does he withhold
  from those whose walk is blameless.

[12]O LORD Almighty,
  blessed is the man who trusts in you.

I HAD ALWAYS KNOWN AMSTERDAM WAS A FASCINATING city though I had never been there. Then we saw advertised the 200th Anniversary of the Rijksmuseum which was to be marked by a special exhibition styled: 'The Golden Age of Dutch Art'. It promised a once in a lifetime gathering together of the best Vermeers and Rembrandts. Add in the prospect of visiting the Van Gogh Museum and we knew we had to go. It was the lure of loveliness. We went and were not disappointed.

All of which is a pale analogy for what the psalmist feels when he contemplates the prospect of going up to Jerusalem for the festival. This song feels like the soundtrack for a promotional video issued by the Zion Tourism Office. But it's not the glories of the Holy City or the splendour of the Temple that is the main attraction. The psalmist longs to meet God. He is enticed by the enchanting presence of his beloved God. He is drawn to the concentrated holiness of God that dwells there. He is lured by the loveliness of God's earthly address.

Adventure (vv.1–4)

Few people live with a sense of destiny or direction until God steps in. When God comes to us, He disturbs our settled patterns of existence. We are made uncomfortable with the humdrum, uneasy with the banal. We have been 'bothered by perfection'.[128] A glimpse of glory has enchanted us and life will never be the same again. We hear an upward call and it is ringing in our hearts as an irresistible summons to God's future.

This is a new experience. It can feel strange to be beckoned to great adventures, summoned to 'get up and leave' as Abraham was from his own country. Your emotions are mixed when you stand on the edge of exploration. Eagerness mingles with edginess. Consumed with new-found hope, your whole body seems to ache with longing (v.2). You have stepped over into what the sociologists call 'the liminal state', the time of transition, the uneasy time betwixt and between the vision and the goal.

So, the psalmist longs intensely for the courts of the Temple where pilgrims lodge at the time of the festival (see Psa. 65:4). His state of mind is similar to that expressed in the songs of aspiration (Psa. 42; 63). His soul yearns, his heart and flesh cry out to know God and to be with Him. He is dreaming God-filled dreams.

In such a mood, even trifling things can stir the heart. A bird's nest is all it takes! Our psalmist thinks of the birds that have made their home in the rafters of the sanctuary or in the clefts of its great stones. And he is envious of their bird's eye view (v.3).

Journey (vv.5-9)

The extraordinary pace of change in our modern Western world has robbed people of any sense of meaning or stable identity. Rabbi Jonathan Sacks comments:

> Something happens when change is so rapid that nothing confers meaning – when lives become lifestyles, commitments become experiments, relationships become provisional, careers turn into contracts, and life itself ceases to have the character of a narrative

and becomes instead a series of episodes with no connecting thread.[129]

Sociologists have characterised people in the post-modern world as vagabonds or tourists in their attitude to the world around them.[130] *Vagabonds* live in reaction to their *past*. They have cut loose from their inherited moorings. They drift through life. They have repudiated their roots and wander history-less and directionless. They are often brave and ironic souls who shrug their indifference at a crazy world: 'Meaningless, meaningless.'

Tourists is what many of us have become in relation to society. Tourists live for the *present* moment. They visit. They do not stay. Everything and everywhere is a hotel not a home. They sample. They do not settle. They accumulate experiences. In his wonderful book of reflections on the Songs of Ascent, Eugene Peterson puts his finger on this state of mind as it has infiltrated the Church.

> Religion in our time has been captured by the tourist mindset. Religion is understood as a visit to an attractive site to be made when we have adequate leisure. Some with a bent for religious entertainment and sacred diversions, plan their lives around special events like retreats, rallies and conferences. We get to see a new personality, to hear a new truth, get a new experience and so, to somehow, expand our otherwise humdrum lives.[131]

But if wanderers live in reaction to the past and tourists live for the present, *pilgrims live towards the future*. This is the biblical vision of the people of God that started with Abraham. Pilgrims are people who are going somewhere. Pilgrims live with a keen sense of direction. They humbly but joyfully believe they are going to God and walking in God's way. They set their sights on God's *'telos'* – the 'end' for which God created and redeemed them. They live in pursuit of this goal. Pilgrims are purpose-driven. They are responding to the upward call of God.

(i) The orientation of the heart is determined by pilgrimage.
The goal or *telos* is written in the pilgrim's heart.
A pilgrim is one 'in whose heart are the highways to Zion' (v.5 NASB). Direction comes not so much from a road map as from an inner compass or computer program. Pilgrims are those who 'have set their hearts on pilgrimage' (v.5 NIV). It is not what they do but what they are. The psalmist's language here echoes the new covenant promise God made to Jeremiah that He would inscribe his 'torah' or 'instruction' on to the very renewed hearts of His people. Walking towards God and His future, walking into His presence and in His ways, has become the habit of the heart.

Jesus was the ultimate pilgrim. In whatever direction He went geographically in his three-year ministry, He was always inwardly on His way to Jerusalem. The title of a famous Lenten sermon by W.E. Sangster is, 'His destination was in His Face'. And it was in His face because it was in His heart.[132]

The psalm celebrates the effects of the pilgrim life.

(ii) The landscape of life is transformed by pilgrimage.
'As they pass through the Valley of Baca, they make it a place of springs' (v.6). The whereabouts of the 'Valley of Baca' is not known. The repointing of the Hebrew word to allow for the translation 'valley of tears' or 'valley of weeping' is attractive but unproven. In view of the next line, the place seems to stand for any arid and parched region through which the pilgrims had to pass. But in difficult and testing terrain God works wonders for those who seek Him. He gives water in the desert. He brings rain in season. Unexpected blessings and surprising grace attend the faithful pilgrim way.

Furthermore, rather than weakening as the upward climb steepens nears its end, the marchers grow stronger in the energy that God supplies (v.7).

Arrival (vv.10–12)

To travel is good; to arrive is better.
The shadow of God's wings have kept the psalmist all the way.
Now, as William Brown puts it, 'on Zion, the Eagle has landed, and so has a people'.[133]
This is the final refuge.
Here is home.

> We shall not cease from exploration
> The end of all our exploring
> Will be to arrive where we started
> And know the place for the first time.[134]

Pilgrims have a wholly different view of the world in which they live. Two comparisons spell this out.

Firstly, *time* is put in true perspective: '*Better* is one day in your courts than a thousand elsewhere' (v.10, own italics).

Modern people talk a lot about finding 'quality time'. It is not so much how long you play with your children after work but what you do with them. 'Invest in quality time' is the mantra. The psalmist is in no doubt: for him every moment spent with God counts for eternity.

Secondly, *work* is set in true proportion: 'I would *rather* be a doorkeeper in the house of my God than dwell in the tents of the wicked' (v.10b, own italics). Gatekeepers at the Temple were not necessarily mere bouncers or ticket collectors! They oversaw judgment on who was allowed entry and who was not.

Pilgrimage is not a lifestyle choice of holiday but an eternal choice of destiny.

Two roads diverged in a wood, and I –
I took the road less traveled
And it has made all the difference[135]

Three times God is described as 'the LORD of hosts' (vv.3, 8, 12 NRSV), the Lord of the 'angel armies' (*The Message*).

- God is the 'living God', fountain of all life, the unquenchable source of vitality (v.2).
- God is the Almighty God and King (v.3). To live in His kingdom is the Good Life.
- God is a sun, the one whose warmth and light makes all life possible (v.11).
- God is our shield of protection (v.11).
- God gives grace and glory (v.11) and he cannot do enough for his own (v.11).

'To draw near to such a God is the *summum bonnum*. Pilgrimage to God's place is a profound symbol of the centering and direction of all life.'[136]

Three Old Testament beatitudes show the way of true blessedness:

- Blessed are those who dwell in God's house (v.4).
- Blessed are those whose strength is in God (v.5).
- Blessed are those who trust in God (v.12).

The God we seek is the Living God and the God we seek seeks us.

One day spent with Him outdoes all other experiences.

A position on His staff however lowly outranks all other occupations.

His habits etched on the heart spell the road to freedom.

His purposes embedded in our souls make commuting to work meaningful.

He is our life in fullness, inspiring singing, imparting strength and bestowing honour.

'My heart and my flesh cry out for the living God …
How lovely is your dwelling-place, O Lord Almighty!'

- To be there in ceaseless praise is to go from song to song (v.4).
- To be on the way there is to go from strength to strength (v.7).
- To be drawn there is to go from glory to glory (v.11).

Be a pilgrim after God. As I and countless millions have discovered, you will not be disappointed.

You can be sure that the Living God, as A.W. Tozer said of the Holy Spirit, 'fully lives up to the advertising'.

'Listen: it grows. The music comes when it is least expected, least deserved, least understood. It is the faint sound that allures us on the journey awaiting the ovation, the rousing applause of heaven.'[137]

Mid-life Crises (Psalm 126)

A song of ascents.

[1]When the LORD brought back the captives to Zion,
  we were like men who dreamed.
[2]Our mouths were filled with laughter,
  our tongues with songs of joy.
Then it was said among the nations,
  'The LORD has done great things for them.'
[3]The LORD has done great things for us,
  and we are filled with joy.

⁴Restore our fortunes, O LORD,
   like streams in the Negev.
⁵Those who sow in tears
   will reap with songs of joy.
⁶He who goes out weeping,
   carrying seed to sow,
will return with songs of joy,
   carrying sheaves with him.

THERE COMES A POINT IN ANY ENTERPRISE – ROUGHLY
mid-way – when progress flags and confidence wanes. At some
stage in any project – including life's journey – doubts can set in
and questions arise. This psalm represents the mid-life crisis not
of an individual but of a community. This can be a time of great
confusion. 'Right there, halfway along our road,' observes Carlo
Carretto, 'we don't know whether we are going backwards or
forwards.'[138] So it was for Israel.

The return to the land after the Babylonian Exile had been an
amazing miracle of grace. But the process of restoration was
proving harder work. Energy-sapping rebuilding, drought, poor
harvests, frustration at the slowness of progress – all these blunted
the edge of enthusiasm.

Psalm 126 releases before God the pent-up weariness and fears.
It's a realistic and reassuring cry.

Lord, reaffirm our past and our future. Was it really like that
then? Can it really be like that again? 'Restore our fortunes, O
LORD' (v.4).

Or as we, a church half-reconstructed, might pray in echo of
ancient Israel: 'Reform the reformation, restore the restoration, O
Lord, renew the renewal.'

Firstly, Lord, we remember how it all began and reaffirm it.

(a) *The first phase was pure joy: joy with laughter* (vv.1–3).
'The Lord has done great things for us, and we are filled with joy.'

'We are glad' as we look back on what God has accomplished. Joy is funded by memory. As Eugene Peterson says: 'Joy has a history. Joy is the verified, repeated experience of those involved in what God is doing. It is as real as a date in history, as solid as a stratum of rock in Palestine. Joy is nurtured by living in such a history, building on its foundation.'[139]

I cast my mind back over thirty years and rejoice.

Lord, you did miracles; You released us from captivity;

You renewed us by marvelous movements of Your Spirit;

You took Your people out of the deep freeze; you freed us from ourselves.

Formal religion felt like an official reception; this was like being at home with You. We let our hair down and put our hands up; we became crazy praisers with 'songs of joy' (v.2).

We discovered you to be a God who, in Spurgeon's words, 'turns exile into ecstasy and banishment into bliss'.

Is anyone still alive who remembers the early 1970s in Britain? Were we not 'like those who dream'?

What dreams were birthed in us then! Dreams of doing big things for God and seeing big things from God; dreams that dwarfed our undernourished expectations of what the Lord could do. And 'our mouth was filled with laughter'. It was the Lord's laughter and it was infectious. So we became carefree too, bold and unabashed. In our small measure, we felt like the disciples for whom the Resurrection 'seemed too good to be true' (Luke 24:41), a prime case of what Oswald Chambers called 'moral hysteria'.

But, as they knew, it 'was too good not to be true!' Perhaps even the world realised something was happening in the Church which sociology alone could not explain (v.2b)? Perhaps, belatedly as usual, the media took notice of the 'happy-clappers' and wondered what was going on among Christians? Or was it only when the tele-evangelists bit the dust that the Church hit the headlines?

One thing for sure: our laughing made us less gullible, less impressed by empty claims, less dependent on human expertise and cleverness, and less able to take ourselves quite so seriously anymore. It's hard to be pompous when faced with God's preposterous miracles! This was what Sarah found when promised Isaac. The initial laughter is sheer disbelief!! Who me? Is this really happening to us? Now?

'The real,' said W.H. Auden, 'is what will strike you as really absurd; unless you are certain you are dreaming, it is certainly a dream of your own; unless you exclaim – "there must be some mistake" – you must be mistaken.'

But when Isaac arrives – whose name means 'laughter' – Sarah goes into the hysterics of amazement, for the joke – God's joke – is now firmly on her!

So we recall the first phase of the renewal of God's people with undiminished gratitude: 'we are (still) glad' (v.3).

For our laughing taught us to expect even more of God, to scorn the parched deserts and dried-up riverbeds of unbelief and to learn how daringly 'faith laughs at impossibilities, and cries "it shall be done"' (Wesley). None of this have we forgotten or disowned. Still for us, the future lies with the dreamers and the laughers, with the leap of faith and the humour of hope.

But we are now into the second phase.

(b) *The second phase is joy with tears* (vv.4–6).
It was always going to be harder. Then everything was done 'for us' by the Lord (v.3): now, what God is doing, is being done by us and through us!

The rebuilding of the Temple and city after the return from Exile is echoed in the psalm.

At one stage the reconstruction work seemed to have stalled. To get it started again it took both Zechariah's enchanting, almost surreal prophecies, and Haggai's down-to-earth directives to 'fetch wood'. Motivated by both prophetic methods – the pictorial and the pragmatic – the workers successfully completed the half-finished project (Ezra 6:14).

The psalmist captures this second stage in agricultural rather than architectural images.

Now is the time not only for singing and dreaming but for sowing and reaping. And the climate is less congenial than it was. Now it is 'out-of-season' work that has to be done. Now the deserts and dried-up riverbeds seem more unyielding than before. We are wearier now, and tempered by experience. The more grandiose prophecies have worn a little thin; the over-blown hype flaps in the wind like an old election poster. The danger at this stage is that those who were once dreamers become disillusioned; the laughter turns to cynicism. Nothing will ever match 'the good old days'.

Culture watcher and theologian, Leonard Sweet, has suggested that comfortable categories which begin with the prefix 're-', hark back nostalgically to a golden era, and must be replaced, in a postmodern world, by 'de-' words.[140]

If this is true then old favourites like 'renewal', 'revival' and – as in this psalm – 'restoration' may need to pass through a deconstruction before wishful thinking is replaced with reality.

None of this spells disillusionment. We need not dismantle all our dreams but we demolish assumptions of easy victories. We do this by accepting that there is no reaping without regular sowing, no return without costly investment. It is to accept that sowing is a kind of dying – hence the tears; that triumphalism laid to rest in the fertile soil of admitted failure bears much fruit! It is, in short, to pray again, 'Restore our fortunes Lord.'

In particular we pray for what is sudden and for what is slower; and for what, in both cases, is sure.

Send the rain, Lord!

'Restore our fortunes ... like streams in the Negev' (v.4).

Just as the winter rains bring sudden flash floods to fill the dried-up wadis of the southern desert, so send the river of your Spirit coursing through our community again! Refresh us, revive us again, re-invigorate us with the rushing waters of mercy and grace.

Give a bumper harvest, Lord!
Give a big return on the investment we've made, Lord.
We have 'sown in tears'; make us 'reap with joy'.
Give a return on the tears we shed at the graveside of the sick child for whom we wept and fasted and prayed but who wasn't among those healed.
Repay with interest what has been stolen from us by the enemy of our souls.
Restore to us with interest the harvest years which the locusts of our own neglect and failure have eaten.
This is our prayer today.
And before we're through, our praying has become prophecy, an assurance born of God's past miracles that 'he who goes out weeping ... will return with songs of joy'. Handfuls of seed yield 'armfuls of blessing' (*The Message*).
This is the lesson of the psalm.
Things may be different now; some dreams are buried by the wayside. The laughter is mellower, more maturely blended with tears. The jokes are subtler and more ironic. The songs sung less loudly because sung from softer hearts. But we are still glad!
'Restore the restoration, O Lord, renew the renewal.'
'The Lord will do great things for us.'
This psalm is one of the songs of ascent. It can be sung still by a pilgrim people, those pressing on past the mid-life crises of the Church, to finish the race.
'He who began a good work in you will bring it to completion at the day of Christ.'
To keep pace with changing times, much may have to be deconstructed in how the Church does things. But to be demoralised is not an option for a pilgrim people. Our motivation is rekindled by a passionate reattachment to the unchanging revolutionary 're-' words of the gospel – redemption and resurrection.

Who would true valour see,
Let him come hither;
One here will constant be,
Come wind, come weather.
There's no discouragement
Shall make him once relent
His first avowed intent
To be a pilgrim.

Joy funded by history and fuelled by hope sustains us for the
journey and the task ahead.

ANTICIPATION

God's Laughter (Psalm 2)

¹Why do the nations conspire
and the peoples plot in vain?
²The kings of the earth take their stand
and the rulers gather together against the LORD
and against his Anointed One.
³'Let us break their chains,' they say,
'and throw off their fetters.'

⁴The One enthroned in heaven laughs;
the Lord scoffs at them.
⁵Then he rebukes them in his anger
and terrifies them in his wrath, saying,
⁶'I have installed my King
on Zion, my holy hill.'

⁷I will proclaim the decree of the LORD:

He said to me, 'You are my Son;
today I have become your Father.
⁸Ask of me,
and I will make the nations your inheritance,
the ends of the earth your possession.
⁹You will rule them with an iron sceptre;
you will dash them to pieces like pottery.'

¹⁰Therefore, you kings, be wise;
be warned, you rulers of the earth.
¹¹Serve the LORD with fear
and rejoice with trembling.
¹²Kiss the Son, lest he be angry
and you be destroyed in your way,
for his wrath can flare up in a moment.
Blessed are all who take refuge in him.

PSALM 2 WAS PROBABLY FIRST SUNG AT THE CORONATION
of a king in Israel. Various participants speak:

- the psalmist paints the scene (vv.1–5)
- God announces His decision (v.6)
- the king affirms his appointment (vv.7–9)
- the psalmist warns the rulers (vv.10–12)

The first voice we hear is that of the psalmist. The prophetic
singer sings of what he sees: the nations in tumultuous assembly,
with their leaders furiously disputing the sovereignty of the world.

vv.1–3 dispute

We are shown that the debate that is raging at this world summit
conference is about how to usurp God's authority and run the
world without God. Such a perception no doubt reflects the fact

that Israel was a political football kicked around by the more powerful teams, whether Egyptian, Assyrian, Babylonian, Persian, Greek, or before long, Roman. The supreme issue is a power struggle that tears the world apart. Whatever their political hue – whether totalitarian or militaristic or democratic – the singer sees all nations as, in effect, seeking to break the chains of submitting to God and His laws (v.3).

In modern times, Nietzsche rightly warned that the rejection of absolute standards would leave a vacuum to be filled by 'the will to power', that is, by those determined enough to seize the power and impose their will on others. For his part, the ancient prophetic singer sees the men of power attempting to carve up God's world into spheres of influence – from which God has been excluded. The particular target for the world's antagonism is the Lord's anointed king (v.2).

v.4 derision

What the psalmist sees and hears next is from an altogether loftier vantage point. He sees the throne in heaven. He is not shown the One reigning from it, but what he hears captures his attention. He hears the sound of derisive laughter emanating from the throne. 'The One enthroned in heaven laughs.' God mocks the pretensions of arrogant men of power and cuts them down to size. As if to say, 'Who on earth do you think you are, believing you can run My world without Me?'

According to sociologist Peter Berger, laughter is one of the 'signals of transcendence'.[141] Laughter raises us above ourselves. It gives us perspective on our circumstances, enables us to see things in true proportion. One of the crimes for which Solzhenitzyn was sent to the Gulag was that he was caught laughing while reading a copy of *Pravda*, the official Soviet Communist newspaper!

And God laughs. In Karl Rahner's view, 'He laughs the laughter of the carefree, the confident, the unthreatened. He laughs the laughter of divine superiority over all the horrible confusion of universal history that is full of blood and torture and insanity and baseness. God laughs. Our God laughs.'[142]

My only disagreement with Rahner is when he goes on to suggest that God gloats over the world's chaos. It is better to reflect with P.T. Forsyth that God 'sits in heaven and laughs. And his smile is inscrutable, and elusive, only not cruel: the smile of endless power and patience, very still, and very secure, and deeply, dimly, kind'.[143]

vv.5–6 decision

As the babble of competing voices fades, the long-neglected voice rises above them all. God declares: 'I have installed my King on Zion, my holy hill' (v.6). Now we begin to understand why the conspiracies and plotting of the godless nations are pointless and 'vain' (v.1). The casting vote is already in! God has already decided who will rule over His world!

The nations are always baffled by this. After all, their empires are grander and vastly more powerful than Israel. Zion is a puny hill, in a little known country in a backwater of the Middle East. How can the king who reigns there in Jerusalem possibly be the ruler of the nations? So God's ways and choices confound the Pharaohs and Nebuchadnezzars. For the 'same reason Caesar Augustus and Pontius Pilate end up as mere footnotes to the royal story of God's Messiah'.[144]

vv.7–9 decree

Now we hear the voice of Israel's king in Jerusalem. As He accedes to the throne, He rehearses the terms of the covenant of kingship originally announced by Nathan to David (2 Sam. 7). He is able as David's successor to apply to Himself the promise made then: He said to me 'You are my Son; today I have become your Father. Ask of me and I will make the nations your inheritance, the ends of the earth your possession …'

If we were to fast-forward the action far enough, we would find two men standing, dripping wet, on a river bank. The heavens immediately open; the Holy Spirit dove-like alights on one of the two men and a voice from heaven – the voice that speaks from the throne – speaks again and says to Him: 'You are my Son.' Whatever else we later learn about Jesus of Nazareth, one thing is sure: from this point on He is God's and Israel's anointed king. He is receiving the throne of His forefather David, as His mother, Mary, had been told. At once He begins announcing that 'God's kingdom is at hand' and urges men and women to enter it.

Almost immediately, again like His predecessor David going out to meet Goliath, he strides out into the desert to confront the personified evil of Satan. Offered all the kingdoms of the world if He will bow down and worship the evil one, He refuses. He knows as God's Son that He is heir to all His Father's estates. He only has to ask for the nations to become His inheritance, the ends of the earth His possession.

When, three years later, He approaches the city where Israel's kings always came to be enthroned, He arrives not as a militaristic warlord but as a gentle king on a donkey. He comes at the last to be crowned not in a palace on Mount Zion but on a cross-shaped throne on Golgotha hill. 'He reigns from the tree.'

Three days later, in a graveyard, a tomb lies empty and open, its stone door pushed aside, attached to which is an old decree, flapping in the breeze: 'You are my Son; today I have become your Father.'

As Paul proclaims to the synagogue worshippers in Antioch, in words which blend 2 Samuel 7:14 and Psalm 2:7, God has fulfilled His promise to the fathers – not least to David – by raising Jesus from the dead; as also it is written in the second psalm 'You are my Son, today I have become your Father' (Acts 13:33ff). The day of His resurrection was the 'today' of His coronation as King when His Sonship was confirmed.

All of this lies beyond the range of the psalmist's vision. It went further than he knew. But the trajectory we have traced from his vision is a true one. The supreme sovereignty of the One Creator

God and the universal lordship of His anointed King and Messiah face the world with an unavoidable choice. That choice is perfectly captured by the psalmist in the closing stanza of his song (vv.10–12).

vv.10–12 discernment

Critical discernment is called for and crucial decisions have to be made which are of life or death importance. A modern video presentation of this would offer us a split screen. On one side the faces of the kings of the earth; on the other the faces of all the King's true subjects. There is a warning for the kings: be wise, be wary, your crowns are about to be taken away, do homage to the Son 'lest he be angry and you be destroyed in your way' (v.12). This is the fate of those who rebel against Him.

But those who take refuge in Him are blessed and shelter under His protection. They have nothing to lose but their sin and shame and failure. The Bible's final vision shows them sharing the sovereignty with the King. Mind you, they never keep their crowns on for very long, for they are always bowing at His feet.

The safety of the world is here and the world's danger.

Your refuge or ruin.

D-Day has Dawned (Psalm 110)

Of David. A psalm.

[1]The LORD says to my Lord:
  'Sit at my right hand
until I make your enemies
  a footstool for your feet.'

[2]The LORD will extend your mighty sceptre from Zion;
  you will rule in the midst of your enemies.
[3]Your troops will be willing
  on your day of battle.
Arrayed in holy majesty,
  from the womb of the dawn
  you will receive the dew of your youth.

[4]The LORD has sworn
  and will not change his mind:
'You are a priest for ever,
  in the order of Melchizedek.'

[5]The LORD is at your right hand;
  he will crush kings on the day of his wrath.
[6]He will judge nations, heaping up the dead
  and crushing the rulers of the whole earth.
[7]He will drink from a brook beside the way;
  therefore he will lift up his head.

THESE ARE TURBULENT AND ANXIOUS DAYS. WORLD
leaders are hidden away in high-level discussions about how to deal
with the violence and hatred in our world. Heads of state and
henchmen of terrorism are pondering their next move. The world
waits for answers to its age-old questions:

- Who really rules the world?
- Is the world out of control?
- Will good ever finally triumph over evil?
- Will truth and righteousness and love at last prevail?

Wouldn't we like to know what's going on in the Oval Office in the White House and how fascinating to be a fly-on-the-wall in the Cabinet Room in Number 10 Downing Street?

In Britain each new leader of the official Opposition Party in Parliament, is immediately made a Privy Councillor so that he or she can be admitted to the inner circle and hear State Secrets! But the biblical writers are even more interested in what is going on in God's Privy Council.

Prophets were those who had privileged access to God's inner sanctum where the key decisions were made that affected the future of the world. False prophets were outsiders, looking and guessing. 'But which of them has stood in the council of the LORD to see or to hear his word ...' (Jer. 23:18, see v.22).

To be a true prophet, on the other hand, was to have inside information on the top-secret thoughts of God – to be taken into God's confidence as He decided the destiny of the nations. So here, a prophetic singer has eavesdropped on God. What he hears he speaks to the king in Israel.

Two things are said to him:

- vv.1–3 'Sit at my right hand ...'
- vv.4–7 'You are a priest for ever ...'

1. The king at God's right hand

God invites the King in Jerusalem to sit with God on the throne of the world, to occupy a place of a supreme honour and majesty as God's right-hand man. God assures the King that all opposition will be routed and every foe vanquished. God promises the King a ready supply of troops who will offer themselves willingly to serve His cause; they will be no reluctant conscript army but an army of eager volunteers. Come D-Day, they will materialise to rally to His banner as mysteriously as the dew of the morning, a holy army with the rising sun glinting on their shields. It is a picture of total victory.

2. *The priest of God's sworn oath*
God swears an unbreakable oath to the King that He will also be a 'priest for ever in the order of Melchizedek'. What is this all about? For one thing, according to the Torah, kingship and priesthood are separate roles. For another, Israel already has a well-established order of priests, the Levites.

But this King is to be different; His priesthood will be forever and of a different order altogether: 'the order of Melchizedek'.

In only one other place in the Old Testament is this character mentioned. Right at the start of the redemptive story, in Genesis 14, a strange figure comes out to meet Abraham; his name is Melchizedek, king of Salem, Salem being the old Jebusite fortress later captured by David and made his capital city, Jerusalem. Not only is Melchizedek a king, he is also a priest, and a priest of 'El Elyon', the Most High God. Abraham, sensing his superiority, pays tithes to him and receives a blessing in return. It is a priest of this kind who will exercise endless mediation.

3. *The judge of God's choice*
This extraordinary and unique priest-king will bring judgment to the wicked and justice to the world; He will rout the malevolent kings and rulers and He will do so in the strength of God Himself (vv.5–6).

Notice the parallel statements here:

- v.1 the Lord at God's right hand
- v.5 God at the king's right hand!

The inspired song ends with the picture of peace and serenity, as the King, replenishing His resources from God's supply, drinks from the streams by the wayside. This picture may echo a now lost part of the coronation ritual (see 1 Kings 1:38–40). In any case, it suggests that the King confidently lifts up His head as the loving master of all He surveys (v.7).

It is a stirring and striking song. But how did it become the favourite psalm of the New Testament writers and the psalm most quoted by the apostles?

Well, the answer starts and ends with Jesus. In the last week before the cross, Jesus famously engages the religious leaders in fierce debate as they furiously react to the evident authority He shows (Matt. 22:41–46). When debating with the Pharisees on the true nature of the Messiah's identity and status, Jesus plays Psalm 110 as His trump card! Do they believe that the Messiah will be a son of David? Of course.

Then, Jesus asks, assuming David to be the author of Psalm 110, as is commonly supposed by this time, how is it that David calls Him 'my lord'? There is far more to the Messiah than meets the expected eye: more to the Messiah than merely being David's son. If David calls Him 'my lord' then He is David's superior … and who knows what that might imply! This threatens to take the idea of messiahship to an altogether higher level, a level that would shatter and rewrite all their preconceptions and threaten their whole control of the situation. Faced with unthinkable conclusions, the Pharisees shut up shop, stop the interrogation and close the debate: 'no longer daring to ask him any more questions' (v.46)!

It was left to the apostles of Jesus to break the silence. After the events of Easter and Ascension, they were in no doubt to whom Psalm 110 applied. They had seen Jesus risen from death, talked with Him, walked with Him, eaten with Him after the resurrection; they had watched Him ascend to the Father; they had been there when, as He promised, the fire from heaven fell and set their hearts aflame with love and shone the bright light of truth into their minds. Now there was no question; no debate was any longer needed: they proclaimed boldly and publicly that God had made Jesus whom they had crucified Messiah of Israel and therefore Lord of the world.

None of this applied to David, they said: David died and his tomb is still with us; David did not ascend to be seated in honour with God; only of Jesus can it be truly said: 'The LORD says to my Lord; "Sit at my right hand until I make your enemies a footstool for your feet"' (Acts 2:34–35).

'The highest place that heaven affords, is his by sovereign right.'

And if we ask what Jesus is doing there as God's right-hand man, ruling and reigning with God, the New Testament writers tell us: He is acting as our Priest, having made the one full and sufficient sacrifice for sins He now prays for us. For 'another priest like Melchizedek appears, one who has become a priest not on the basis of a regulation as to his ancestry but on the basis of the power of an indestructible life'. For it is declared: "You are a priest for ever, in the order of Melchizedek"' (Heb. 7:16–17).

The Levitical priests kept things in their family: Jesus was from outside that family. They died and had to be replaced: He lives in the mighty power of a resurrected life that can never die and so needs never to be replaced. He is our priest for ever! For ever He lives to make intercession for us.

Jesus is the perfect go-between: He brings sinful humanity into a permanent relationship with the Holy God by an unrepeatable sacrifice of Himself and by ceaseless prayer for others. He makes our peace. He makes us whole. He keeps us good!

In the end He has the power and persistence to win back the world for the Father and His kingdom and to defeat our final enemy which is death itself: 'Then the end will come, when he hands over the kingdom to God the Father after he has destroyed all dominion, authority and power. For he must reign until he has put all his enemies under his feet. The last enemy to be destroyed is death' (1 Cor. 15:24–26).

Will the scourge of death finally be swept from God's world?

Will the shadow of death one day never again fall across our path?

Yes, yes, yes – declare the apostles: Jesus is risen from the dead, and He must reign as our priest-king until even the last enemy – death – yields to His rule of love!

When the world rocks on its foundation, when events are dark and foreboding, then we find out what faith's true foundation is. Too often our Christianity is much too self-absorbed. We seek after spiritual experiences to make our lives a bit more successful and to feel better about ourselves. But in times like this such self-centredness in spiritual things counts for nothing. When it comes to the world's salvation, what matters most is what God says, and what God swears to do. And what saves the world is what God says and swears to do – for someone else! This is our gospel: not first of all what God has done for us or will do for us to make our lives more complete; our gospel is about what God has done to Jesus. Everything else flows from that supreme reality.

- God has made this Jesus whom you crucified Christ and Lord of all nations.
- God has taken this Jesus whom men discredited and given Him the seat of honour beside Himself.
- God has given all authority to this Jesus.
- God has made this Priest's sacrifice and endless intercession the lasting salvation of the world forever.

And what of the people He heads? *Isn't the world looking for a people who represent His strange way of priestly kingship?* The oracle to the King echoes the original human vocation to share God's dominion and bring everything 'under his feet' (v.1, see Gen. 1:26–28; Psa. 8). He is summoned as the Truly Human One who will in time bring many sons to His own glory. Meanwhile He stamps on them again the priest-king's indelible image of true humanness.

Believers 'awarded the Order of Melchizedek … are called …

not to fight fire with fire, terrorism with terrorism, rationalism with perfect rationalism, split-second communication that superficialises with still quicker, lightning-like communication. The royal priesthood is directed to fight fire with the water of forgiveness lest we have only a scorched earth left'.[145]

Doesn't the world long for a true and perfect king; a righteous and benevolent ruler who will eradicate evil from our world? George W. Bush spoke wistfully, like so many mighty men before and after ridding the world of evil; but they will never do it. Only one person has the means and the credentials, the God-given right and God-bestowed power to do so; only to His lordship will the malignant enemies of God's good creation finally submit. Only one community has the gift to embody this.

Isn't the world desperate for a peacemaker, for a priest to heal its wounds, for someone to put together its brokenness, to reconcile its warring factions, to reconcile us all to the One Creator God who made us? But only one priest has the depth of loving self-sacrifice and limitless patience of resurrected persistence to set the world to rights and make a new creation by His once for all cross and always for ever intercession. Only one priesthood has the incentive to keep paying the price of this vision.

Can't you hear the cries of the oppressed across the earth for justice? For an end to tyranny and exploitation, for a reign of righteousness and peace? 'Infinite justice' was how the American President styled it after September 11th 2001. It was an unfortunate phrase, but we didn't need Muslims to query this; we too protest that only God can dispense 'infinite justice' and this is just what Jesus does.

- Jesus is our Priest-King.
- He alone achieves total victory.
- He alone by endless mediation provides permanent peace.
- He alone establishes infinite justice.

To Him shall every knee bow and every tongue will confess Him 'Lord' to the glory of God the Father. Only He has the secret of a new world order for the nations in turmoil; only He has the secret of new creation life for all who bow the knee in repentance and faith and confess Him as their one and only Lord.

It is not for us to decide whether the Lord is King or not; we have only to decide whether we stand with God's enemies among whom He rules, or whether, as willing recruits, we volunteer freely to enlist in His cause.

Gospel Song (Psalm 96)

¹Sing to the LORD a new song;
    sing to the LORD, all the earth.
²Sing to the LORD, praise his name;
    proclaim his salvation day after day.
³Declare his glory among the nations,
    his marvellous deeds among all peoples.

⁴For great is the LORD and most worthy of praise;
    he is to be feared above all gods.
⁵For all the gods of the nations are idols,
    but the LORD made the heavens.
⁶Splendour and majesty are before him;
    strength and glory are in his sanctuary.

⁷Ascribe to the LORD, O families of nations,
    ascribe to the LORD glory and strength.
⁸Ascribe to the LORD the glory due to his name;
    bring an offering and come into his courts.
⁹Worship the LORD in the splendour of his holiness;
    tremble before him, all the earth.

[10]Say among the nations, 'The LORD reigns.'
  The world is firmly established, it cannot be moved;
  he will judge the peoples with equity.
[11]Let the heavens rejoice, let the earth be glad;
  let the sea resound, and all that is in it;
[12] let the fields be jubilant, and everything in them.
Then all the trees of the forest will sing for joy;
[13] they will sing before the LORD, for he comes,
  he comes to judge the earth.
He will judge the world in righteousness
  and the peoples in his truth.

IN HIS GENTLY IRONIC ASSESSMENT OF ENGLISH CULTURE, *England, An Elegy*, the social philosopher, Roger Scruton, writes wryly of a native folk religion in which God is 'an Englishman, uncomfortable in the presence of enthusiasm, reluctant to make a fuss, but trapped into making public speeches'. Typically in charming and well-polished village churches, Scruton reflects, not unkindly, 'God had moved with stiff English decorum ... had played the part of host to generations of people whose shyness He respected and shared'.[146]

To all such reticence, however well meaning, Psalm 96 is a powerful counterblast!

'Sing, sing, sing ...' it urges us three times in its passionate introit!

'Sing to the LORD a new song; sing to the LORD, all the earth. Sing to the LORD, praise his name.'

In short: For heaven's sake, sing!

Something more, then, is called for here than a low murmur of approval of a God-seeking re-election from His undemanding and undemonstrative constituents.

Psalm 96 calls for powerful prophetic praise which evokes:

• the newness of God (vv.1–5)

- the 'nowness' of God (vv.5–9)
- the nearness of God (vv.10–13)

The key to the whole psalm is the 'new song' sung to Yahweh, the Covenant LORD of Israel (v.1).

R.S. Thomas, in his famous poem, *Welsh landscape*, mourns, with bittersweet words, the dying of Wales, a land 'brittle with relics, wind-bitten towers and castles, with sham ghosts ...' inhabited by a people 'sick with inbreeding, worrying the carcass of an old song'.[147]

How did William Williams' great paeon of praise to the eighteenth-century revival, 'Guide me O thou great Jehovah', come to echo around Cardiff Arms Park, or more recently the Millenium Stadium, as the rallying song of Welsh rugby?

How odd that Toplady's intensely pietistic 'Abide with me' should preface the English Football's Cup Final lately at Wembley – so bizarrely disconnected from the evangelical fervour which inspired it.

The 'new song' is what we need!

(a) *The 'new song' prophetically recalls the past salvation achieved by God (vv.1–5).*

What is a 'new song'?
Not merely a fresh composition from the pens of imaginative songwriters. This is not about whether we prefer our hymns ancient or modern or a blend of both. This has nothing directly to do with so-called 'worship wars' between traditional and contemporary worship styles. But then perhaps it does.

It does if we begin to make the vital connection between the 'new song' of verse 1 and the new news proclaimed in praise in verse 2.

The verb 'proclaim' (v.2) is the Hebrew word *'basar'* which means to 'proclaim the news'. This is the word root for the term 'good tidings' or 'gospel' (see Isa. 40:9; 52:7).

The 'new song' originated in military contexts as the news of victory on the battlefield (see Psa. 144:1–10). Tremper Longman III and Daniel Reid conclude: 'It appears that new song is a technical term for victory song. These songs celebrate the new situation brought about by God's warring activity.' [148]

Walter Brueggemann suggests that over time the phrase lost its explicitly military connotation and came to stand for a celebration of God's saving actions. These ranged from the national to the domestic. A new song could be public praise of what the nation's saviour had done, or could express the personal thanks of individuals to the God who saves, heals and delivers – what Brueggemann calls 'drastic verbs on the lips of little people'. [149]

The gospel is proclaimed when news of God's saving victory is passed from one place to another place and from one time to another time. In this way the original impact of God's triumph is transmitted to a different audience and location who are made to feel afresh the immediate presence of a saving God. Praise is prophetic and worship is sacramental for this very reason; God's salvation in the past is made vitally present in the here and now! This is the significance of singing a 'new song'.

So a 'new song' is not necessarily a new lyric but an old song which recalls the saving deeds of God in the past which are renewed with fresh meaning and impact as God is praised as the One who saves. None of this involves novelty or gimmicks or strained attempts at relevance. What the new song does is to 'to report the victory of God wrought elsewhere that has decisive effect on the situation in which the reported outcome is spoken and heard'. [150] This is true 'gospel music'.

Receiving the 'news' removes fear, assuages grief, creates happiness and may trigger riotous and wild celebrations! (see Nahum 1:15).

True praise is always gospel-centred – so that singing, praising, and preaching directs us to the God whose saving love in the past is freshly evoked and enjoyed and applauded!

'Tell me the old, old story.' 'Tell me the story freshly ...' The remembered story of our covenant Lord dawns afresh on the consciousness of the worshippers.

We celebrate the newness of our God and of His love. Even in the darkest times, we can sing the Lord's great compassions 'are new every morning; great is your faithfulness' (Lam. 3:21).

The news breaks again and again of our saving God.

(b) *The 'new song' prophetically declares His present Lordship* (vv.5–10). Proclaim over the entire world of nations, summon the whole to declare (vv.1,3,7) this one great message: 'The LORD reigns' (v.10).

'The Lord reigns.' This is our 'new song'. Not the tired old songs of a world grown weary with the mismanagement of it by the false gods of power and wealth and self-interested wisdom but the 'new song' evoked by the presence of God among us. Even old words will do provided they are sung with new feelings and fresh affections (Matthew Henry).

Our song dethrones the false gods, topples the idols, demystifies the secret regimes, delegitimises the current ruling powers, relativises all other authority, and re-orders the world for God's glory. Our worship reorientates it around Yahweh, recentres it on His sovereignty and realigns it with His loving will. The world is symbolically re-established on firm foundations (v.10). Infinite justice and final fairness are pronounced as possible for our world (v.10b).

The singing of a new song and the proclamation of news of God's salvation contemporise His Godness so that His splendour and majesty are felt 'before him' as in His very presence. His strength and glory are known right here 'in his sanctuary' (v.6). The effect upon us as we worship in the sanctuary is life-changing and healing. We meet with our God again! We bring our shame and disgrace and bathe our lives in the sparkling splendour of our God. We come with the hunched shoulders of people borne down by the pressure of lesser authorities and we straighten up. Enthralled, we lift up our heads and hearts (and hands too, hopefully) as we gaze upon His ultimate majesty. We offer our weakness and it is made perfect in His strength. We expose the tawdriness and ugliness of our failures and motives and we are dazzled by a sight of His beauty.

Our God reigns!
This is a statement of our faith. God's kingship, which is secure in the heavens where angels and archangels ceaselessly affirm it around the throne, is daringly and audaciously asserted by the prophetic worshippers in a world that seems daily in denial of it! This 'proclamation of God's reign is made before all the evidence is in: it is eschatological'.[151]

If the world has no story to tell and live by, then all is lost, everything is random, all meaning dissolves. Without narrative thread we have no history and no destiny. But we sing to the world a 'new song' and invite it, indeed summon it to join in. 'Ascribe to the LORD, O families of nations ... glory and strength' (vv.7-9). Worship overspills into witness. Proclamation in praise births proclamation in evangelism. We have a story to tell to the nations. Our praise invites the world to step in that saving story. The 'shout of the King is among them' (Num. 23:21). 'The Lord reigns' now!

(c) *The 'new song' prophetically anticipates what God is about to do and beginning to do and planning to do to shape the future (vv.11-13).* 'The Lord is coming' is the 'new song'! This too is the ultimate in 'good news'. It is the prophet Isaiah (Isa. 42:9-10) who links the 'new thing' God is about to do with the 'new song' believers are invited to sing! In the prophet's case it was the dramatic return from Exile achieved by the mysterious ways of God. So extraordinary would this act of deliverance be that it would even eclipse the original Exodus act of salvation!

In the 'new song' we celebrate God's future; we sing out what the prophets are seeing and hearing and sensing God is doing or is about to do!

Such praise stirs our dreams and visions and longings: it allows us space to bring our questions and to invite God to come into the shortfall between our promises and our performance. As we bring our broken dreams we invite God to inhabit the space between His promises and their fulfilment. So we do not lose heart. The 'new song' looks forward to and draws into the present the future of the kingdom. The 'new song' enables us to live with hope, with fortitude and with patience as we reach out for the world of justice and peace which is yet to come. On behalf of others we sing and pray: 'Your kingdom come, O Lord' and reach out for the coming of the God who is coming to meet us.

Singing the 'new song' is a counter-cultural act. Marshal Macluhan said once that bad news was news and good news is advertising! Furthermore not only are we suspicious of 'good news' but round the clock saturation coverage of news media numbs our appreciation for what is really newsworthy.

Broadcaster and theologian, Colin Morris, coined the term 'newszak' for this paralysing avalanche of news. Newszak is to news what muzak is to music. Muzak is all that is left of music when its performance ceases to be an occasion and becomes a background, an interminable flood of sound, fitfully recognisable, that floats in and out of our consciousness. Muzak is the husk of music, what remains after its emotional power has been discharged. It is still serviceable in a society which cannot stand, or is not allowed to have, silence. Newszak is the husk of news – events drained of topicality, moments evacuated of their original horror, splendour or interest, sensations that have lost the sting of their first impact but still make pretty or shocking pictures ...[152]

But nothing remains untouched by the 'new song'.
- The sanctuary fills with His glory (v.6).
- The nations tremble at His holiness (v.9).
- The whole creation resounds with joy (vv.11–12).

'To commune with the Presence is to be in at the end and at the center where the world is whole, fresh, and always issuing new from the Father's hand through Christ in the Spirit.'[153]

'In short,' concludes Clinton McCann,

a decision must be made. Can we, shall we 'sing to the Lord a new song' amid the same old daily realities' – those pressures that grind us down, that sameness that induces boredom or resignation?

Can we, shall we say, 'the Lord reigns' when the forces of evil seem overpowering?

Can we, shall we say 'the world is firmly established' when things around us seem to be falling apart?

Can we, shall we wait for the Lord and the establishment of his justice?

We can, we shall, we must.[154]

So we sing our 'new song'.

As we do, God's past victories are made over again to us in the here and now; His permanent heavenly rule is made present with us here and now and the prospect of His future kingdom encourages us to break ranks and to start cheering here and now as we wait without illusion but with hope and patience for God's better world to come. As we do we encounter the newness and 'nowness' and nearness of our reigning Lord.

Weather Outlook

To be sure, it feels wintry enough still; but often in the very early spring it feels like that.

The spring comes slowly down this way; but the great thing is that the corner has been turned. There is of course, this difference, that in the natural spring the crocus cannot choose whether it will respond or not. We can. We have the power either of withstanding the spring, and sinking back into the cosmic winter, or of going on into those 'high mid-summer pomps' in which our Leader, the Son of Man, already dwells, and to which He is calling us. It remains with us to follow or not, to die in this winter, or to go on into that spring and that summer.[155]

Prayer and Reflections

Lord I am thirsty for You.
I crave the sense of Your presence.
I am hungry for Your love.
I have glimpsed Your glory and tasted Your goodness and I know
   that nothing else satisfies my soul as You do.

Lord stir me to press on in response to Your upward call in
   Christ Jesus.
Keep alive in me a pilgrim spirit and may Your ways increasingly
   become the habits of my heart.

My eyes have seen the King.
The sun has risen on Your coming kingdom.
The dawn is part of the morning that is certain to follow.
Renew my hope in You, Lord, not as a fleeting optimism but
   as a fixity of gaze and purpose.
Give me the outlook of the kingdom on all things and make me
   willing to pay the price of the vision.
Through Jesus Christ our current Lord and coming King.
Amen.

- Consider again Larry Crabb's three levels of longing mentioned in the meditation on Psalm 42 – casual, crucial and critical and use them to do a stock-check on your own desire for God.

- Make a list of those special times when you have known the Lord's presence and power in your life whether on your own or in public worship.

- Retrace your own spiritual journey and seek to discover what difficulties now impede your spiritual progress as compared to previous years.

- Compose a statement of intent in which you resolve from this moment on to trust God more.

- Consider what overall impact the Psalms have had on you as you have studied them again. How useful is the 'four seasons' idea for helping you meditate on them, and how might you turn to the Psalms in a new way in the future to help you in your walk with God?

Notes

1. Kathleen Norris, *The Cloister Walk* (Oxford: Lion Books, 1999) p.113.

2. Philip Yancey, 'How I Learned to Stop Hating and Start Loving the Psalms', *Christianity Today*, 6 October 1989.

3. Eugene Peterson, *Answering God: The Psalms as Tools for Prayer* (San Francisco: Harper and Row, 1989) Chapter Three.

4. Kathleen Norris, *The Cloister Walk* (Oxford: Lion Books, 1999) p.119.

5. Martin E. Marty, *A Cry of Absence: Reflections for the Winter of the Heart* (San Francisco: Harper and Row, 1983) pp.35–6.

6. The story is told by Donald McCullough, *The Trivialisation of God* (Colorado: NavPress, 1995) pp.115–16.

7. Exodus 19–24 and see further Philip Greenslade, *A Passion for God's Story* (Carlisle: Paternoster, 2002) pp.87–108.

8. Eugene Peterson, *Answering God: The Psalms as Tools for Prayer* (San Francisco: Harper and Row, 1989) p.91.

9. Ronald B. Allen, *Praise A Matter of Life and Breath: Praising God in the Psalms* (Nashville: Nelson, 1980) p.26.

10. Tremper Longman III, *How To Read the Psalms* (Downers Grove: IVP, 1988) p.91.

11. Kathleen Norris quoted William P. Brown, *Seeing The Psalms: A Theology of Metaphor* (Louisville: Westminster John Knox Press) p.12.

12. Paul Ricoeur quoted by William P. Brown in op. cit. p.2.

13. Ronald B. Allen, *Praise! A Matter of Life and Breath: Praising God in the Psalms* (Nashville: Nelson, 1980) p.51.

14. Craig Broyles, *Psalms, New International Biblical Commentary* (Peabody: Hendrickson, 1999) p.31.

15. Gerald H. Wilson, 'Psalms and Psalter, Paradigm for Biblical Theology' in ed. Scott J. Hafemann, *Biblical Theology, Retrospect and Prospect* (Downers Grove: IVP, 2002) pp.105–6.

16. Walter Brueggemann, *Israel's Praise: Doxology against Idolatry and Ideology* (Minneapolis: Fortress Press, 1988) p.160.

17. Ronald B. Allen, *Praise! A Matter of Life and Breath: Praising God in the Psalms* (Nashville: Nelson, 1980) p.26.

18. Eugene Peterson, *Answering God: The Psalms as Tools for Prayer* (San Francisco: Harper and Row, 1989) pp.3, 5.

19. J. Clinton McCann, *A Theological Introduction to the Book of Psalms* (Nashville: Abingdon Press, 1993) pp.25–7.

20. Ibid., p.27.

21. James L. Mays, *The Lord Reigns, A Theological Handbook to the Psalms* (Louisville: Westminster John Knox Press, 1994) p.122.

22. J. Clinton McCann, *A Theological Introduction to the Book of Psalms* (Nashville: Abingdon Press, 1993) pp.27, 48.

23. Barbara Green, *Like a Tree Planted: An Exploration of Psalms and Parables Through Metaphor* (Collegeville: The Liturgical Press, 1997) p.30.

24. J. Clinton McCann, *A Theological Introduction to the Book of Psalms* (Nashville: Abingdon Press, 1993) p.35.

25. William P. Brown, *Seeing the Psalms: A Theology of Metaphor* (Louisville: Westminster John Knox Press, 2002) p.46.

26. Ibid., p.46.

27. Ibid., p.27.

28. Ibid., p.28.

29. Ibid., p.45.

30. Ibid., p.48.

31. Ibid., p.45.

32. Ibid., p.52.

33. Claus Westermann, *The Praise of God in the Psalms* (London: Epworth Press, 1965) p.22.

34. Don Saliers, *Worship Come to its Senses* (Nashville: Abingdon Press, 1996) p.65. Also see the subtitle of a volume of essays in tribute to Saliers' work, *Liturgy and the Moral Self: Humanity at Full Stretch Before God* (Collegeville: The Liturgical Press, 1998).

35. Ronald B. Allen, *Praise! A Matter of Life and Breath: Praising God in the Psalms* (Nashville: Thomas Nelson, 1980).

36. Claus Westermann, *The Praise of God in the Psalms* (London: Epworth Press, 1965) p.159.

37. J. Clinton McCann, *A Theological Introduction to the Book of Psalms* (Nashville: Abingdon Press, 1993) p.56.

38. George Herbert, 'Providence' in *The Poems Of George Herbert, The World's Classics* (London: Oxford University Press, 1958) p.105.

39. William P. Brown, *Seeing the Psalms: A Theology of Metaphor* (Louisville: Westminster John Knox Press, 2002) p.162.

40. Gerald H. Wilson, *Psalms Volume One, NIV Application Series* (Grand Rapids: Zondervan, 2002) p.573. See also p.535.

41. Ibid., p.573. See also p.535.

42. Walter Brueggemann, ed. Patrick Miller, *The Psalms and the Life of Faith* (Minneapolis: Fortress Press, 1995) p.114.

43. Ibid., p.114.

44. Daniel Hardy and David Ford, *Jubilate: Theology in Praise* (London: Darton, Longman, and Todd, 1984) p.81.

45. Ibid., p.82.

46. James L. Mays, *Psalms: Interpretation Series* (Louisville: John Knox Press, 1994) p.331.

47. Calvin Seerveld, *Rainbows for the Fallen World* (Toronto: Tuppence Press, 1980) p.23.

48. Gerard Manley Hopkins, 'God's Grandeur', *The Complete Poems with Selected Prose* (London: Fount, 1996) p.18.

49. Annie Dillard, *Pilgrim at Tinker Creek* (New York: Harper-Collins, 1974) p.135.

50. Ibid., p.146.

51. Walter Brueggemann, *Israel's Praise: Doxology against Idolatry and Ideology* (Minneapolis: Fortress Press, 1988) p.1.

52. Patrick D. Miller, *They Cried to the Lord* (Minneapolis: Fortress Press, 1994) p.223.

53. Walter Brueggemann, ed. Patrick Miller, *The Psalms and the Life of Faith* (Minneapolis: Fortress Press, 1995) p.117.

54. Patrick D. Miller, *They Cried to the Lord* (Minneapolis, Fortress Press, 1994) p.224.

55. Claus Westermann, *The Praise of God in the Psalms* (London: Epworth Press, 1965) pp.22–3.

56. Walter Brueggemann, *The Message of the Psalms* (Minne-apolis: Augsburg Press, 1984) pp.19–23.

57. Gerald H. Wilson, *Psalms Volume One, NIV Application Series* (Grand Rapids: Zondervan, 2002) p.532.

58. John Piper, *The Purifying Power of Living by Faith in Future Grace* (Leicester: IVP, 1995) pp.31–9.

59. John Piper, *Desiring God: Meditations of a Christian Hedonist* (Portland: Multnomah, 1986) p.140.

60. Claus Westermann, *The Praise of God in the Psalms* (London: Epworth Press, 1965) p.25; Ronald B. Allen, *Praise a Matter of Life and Breath: Praising God in the Psalms* (Nashville: Nelsoon, 1980) pp.63, 168.

61. Harvey Guthrie, *Theology as Thanksgiving, From Israel's Praise to the Church's Eucharist* (New York: The Seabury Press, 1981) p.24.

62. Herbert Butterfield, *Writings on Christianity and History* (New York: Oxford University Press, 1979) p.79.

63. W.H. Auden: 'In memory of W.B.Yeats' in *Collected Shorter Poems, 1927–1957* (London: Faber and Faber Ltd, 1966) p.143.

64. P.T. Forsyth, *The Taste of Death and The Life of Grace* (London: James Clarke, 1901) p.74.

65. Horatius Bonar, nineteenth-century pastor, theologian and hymnwriter.

66. Derek Kidner, *Psalms 1–72* and *Psalms 73–150* (London: IVP, 1975).

67. Walter Brueggemann, *The Message of the Psalms* (Minne-apolis: Augsburg, 1984) p.90.

68. John Piper, *The Purifying Power of Living by Faith in Future Grace* (Leicester: IVP, 1995) pp.33, 39.

69. John Piper, *Desiring God: Meditations of a Christian Hedonist* (Portland: Multnomah, 1986) p.140.

70. Hans-Joachim Kraus, *Psalms 1–59* (Minneapolis: Fortress Press, 1993) p.490.

71. P.T. Forsyth, *The Justification of God* (London: Independent Press, 1917/1948) p.207.

72. P.T. Forsyth, *Missions in State and Church* (London: Hodder & Stoughton, 1908) p.44.

73. Martin Marty, *A Cry of Absence: Reflections for the Winter of the Heart* (San Francisco: Harper and Row, 1983) pp.12–21. Marty attributes the phrase to Karl Rahner.

74. Ibid., p.21.

75. Paul Ricoeur, *Figuring The Sacred* (Minneapolis: Fortress Press, 1995) pp.60–61.

76. Judith Gundry-Volf and Miroslav Volf, *A Spacious Heart: Essays on Identity and Belonging* (Harrisburg: Trinity Press International, 1997) p.56.

77. Larry Silva, 'The Cursing Psalms as a Source of Blessing' in ed. Stephen Breck Reid, *Psalms and Practice: Worship,Virtue, and Authority* (Collegeville: The Liturgical Press, 2001) p.221.

78. Ibid., p.222.

79. Ellen Davis, *Getting Involved With God: Rediscovering the Old Testament* (Cambridge: Cowley Publications, 2001) p.28.

80. Rolf Jacopson, 'Burning our Lamps with Borrowed Oil: The Liturgical Use of the Psalms and The Life of Faith', in ed. Stephen Breck Reid, *Psalms and Practice: Worship, Virtue and Authority* (Collegeville: The Liturgical Press, 2001) pp.90–98.

81. Walter Brueggemann, ed. Patrick Miller, *The Psalms and the Life of Faith* (Minneapolis: Fortress Press, 1995) p.102.

82. C.H. Spurgeon, *Twelve Sermons On Thanksgiving* (Grand Rapids: Baker Book House, 1982) pp.18–19.

83. Ted Peters, *Sin: Radical Evil in Soul and Society* (Grand Rapids: Eerdmans, 1994) p.9.

84. C.S. Lewis, *Letters to Malcolm Chiefly on Prayer* (London: Geoffrey Bles, 1964) p.94.

85. Emil Brunner, *Man in Revolt* (London: Lutterworth Press, 1947) p.136.

86. Ted Peters, *Sin: Radical Evil in Soul and Society* (Grand Rapids: Eerdmans, 1994) p.327.

87. Walter Brueggemann, *The Message of the Psalms* (Minne-apolis: Augsburg Press, 1984) pp.100–1.

88. Derek Kidner, *Psalms 1–72* (London: IVP, 1973) p.192.

89. Ellen Davis, *Getting Involved With God: Rediscovering the Old Testament* (Cambridge: Cowley Publications, 2001) p.168.

90. James L. Mays, *Psalms: Interpretation Series* (Louisville: John Knox Press, 1994) p.203.

91. Kathryn L. Roberts, *Psalms and Practice: Worship, Vision and Authority* (Collegeville: The Liturgical Press, 2001) p.104.

92. Kathleen Norris, *Amazing Grace: A Vocabulary of Faith* (New York: Riverhead Books, 1998) p.165.

93. P.T. Forsyth, *Revelation, Old and New* (London: Independent Press, 1962).

94. D.M. Lloyd-Jones, *Revival: Can we make it happen?* (Basing-stoke: Marshall Pickering, 1986) p.193.

95. G.K. Chesterton, *Orthodoxy* (London: John Lane, the Bodley Head, 1927) pp.106–7.

96. D.M. Lloyd-Jones, *Revival: Can we make it happen?* (Basing-stoke: Marshall Pickering, 1986) pp.90–91.

97. William P. Brown, *Seeing the Psalms: A Theology of Metaphor* (Louisville: Westminster John Knox Press, 2002) p.182.

98. Walter Brueggemann, *Peace* (St Louis: Chalice Press, 2001).

99. Walter Brueggemann, *Theology of the Old Testament* (Minne-apolis: Fortress Press, 1997) p.224.

100. Walter Brueggemann, *Peace* (St Louis: Chalice Press, 2001) p.6.

101. A.W. Tozer, *The Pursuit of God* (London: Marshall, Morgan & Scott, 1961) p.14.

102. Daniel Hardy and David Ford, *Jubilate: Theology in Praise* (London: Darton, Longman and Todd) p.138.

103. John Piper, *The Purifying Power of Living by Faith in Future Grace* (Leicester: IVP, 1995) p.9.

104. John Piper, *Desiring God* (Oregon: Multnomah, 1986) p.38.

105. Ibid., pp.69–70.

106. Ibid., p.113.

107. John Piper, *God's Passion for God's Glory* (Leicester; IVP, 1998) p.36.

108. John Eldredge: *The Journey of Desire* (Nashville: Nelson, 2000) p.11.

109. Ben Witherington, *Jesus the Sage* (Edinburgh: T&T Clark, 1994) p.249.

110. Martin Hengel, 'Hymns and Christology' in *Between Jesus and Paul* (London: SCM Press, 1983) pp.78–96.

111. Ibid., p.95.

112. Ellen Davis, *Getting Involved With God: Rediscovering the Old Testament* (Cambridge: Cowley Publications, 2001) p.37.

113. Walter Brueggemann, ed. Patrick Miller, *The Psalms and the Life of Faith* (Minneapolis: Fortress Press, 1995) p.51.

114. Larry Crabb, *Inside Out* (Colorado: NavPress 1998) pp.80–88.

115. James L. Mays, *Psalms, Interpretation Series* (Louisville: John Knox Press, 1994) p.173.

116. Antoine de Saint-Exupéry, *The Little Prince* (Middlesex: Penguin Books, 1965).

117. Martyn Lloyd-Jones, *Spiritual Depression: Its Causes and Cure* (London: Pickering & Inglis, 1965) p.20.

118. Abraham Heschel, *Man is not Alone* (New York: The Noonday Press, 1951) p.259.

119. A.W. Tozer, *The Pursuit of God* (London: Marshall, Morgan & Scott, 1961) p.7.

120. Cited by Richard Winter, *Still Bored in a Culture of Entertainment: Rediscovering Passion and Wonder* (Downers Grove: IVP, 2002) p.49.

121. Ibid., p.133.

122. As told by Brennan Manning, *The Ragamuffin Gospel* (Oregon: Multnomah, 1990) pp.18–19.

123. David Wells, *God in the Wasteland: The Reality of Truth in a World of Fading Dreams* (Grand Rapids: Eerdmans, 1994) pp.88–117.

124. For the language of the whole paragraph see ibid., p.88.

125. Frederick William Faber, 'Desire of God' in *Hymns* (London: Burns and Oates Ltd, 1861) pp.282–3.

126. A.W. Tozer, *The Pursuit of God* (London: Marshall, Morgan & Scott, 1961) p.15.

127. John Piper, *God's Passion for His Glory* (Leicester: IVP, 1998) p.41.

128. Thomas Howard, *One Upon a Time, God …* (London: Lakeland, 1974) p.60.

129. Jonathan Sacks, *The Dignity of Difference* (New York: Continuum, 2003) p.75.

130. Zygmunt Bauman quoted in Sacks, *The Dignity of Difference* (New York: Continuum, 2003) p.76.

131. Eugene Peterson, *A Long Obedience in the Same Direction* (Downers Grove: IVP, 1980) p.12.

132. W.E. Sangster, *Westminster Sermons* (London: Epworth Press, 1961) p.61.

133. William Brown, *Seeing The Psalms: A Theology of Metaphor* (Louisville: Westminster John Knox Press, 2002) p.23.

134. T.S. Eliot, 'Little Gidding', *Four Quartets* (London: Faber & Faber, 1959) p.59.

135. Robert Frost, 'The Road Not Taken', in *Robert Frost Selected Poems* (Middlesex: Penguin Books, 1962) p.78.

136. James L. Mays, *Psalms: Interpretation Series* (Louisville: John Knox Press, 1994) p.275.

137. Dan Allender and Tremper Longman III, *The Cry of the Soul* (Christchurch: NavPress, 1995) p.259.

138. Carlo Carretto, *Letters From The Desert* (London: Darton, Longman & Todd, 1972) p.65.

139. Eugene Peterson, *A Long Obedience in the Same Direction* (Downers Grove: IVP, 1980) p.95.

140. Leonard Sweet, *Soultsunami* (Grand Rapids: Zondervan, 1999) pp.147ff.

141. Peter L. Berger, *A Rumour of Angels* (Middlesex; Penguin Books, 1969) pp.70, 89.

142. Karl Rahner, *The Eternal Year* (London: Burns and Oates, 1964) p.53.

143. P.T. Forsyth, *The Justification of God* (London: Independent Press, 1917/ reptd 1948) p.204.

144. Philip Greenslade, *Passion for God's Story* (Carlisle: Pater-noster, 2002) p.116. Chapter 6 of this book shows how Psalm 2 fits into the story of the Davidic Covenant and, in turn, into the larger redemptive plan of God.

145. Calvin Seerveld, *On Being Human* (Ontario: Welch Publish-ing Co., 1988) p.83.

146. Roger Scruton, *England, An Elegy* (London: Pimlico, 2001) pp.91–2.

147. R.S. Thomas, 'Welsh Landscape', *Collected Poems 1945–1990* (London: Phoenix, 1999) p.37.148.   Tremper Longman III and Daniel Reid, *God is a Warrior* (Carlisle: Paternoster, 1995) p.45.

149. Walter Brueggemann, *Israel's Praise* (Philadelphia: Fortress Press, 1988) p.151. I am heavily indebted to Brueggemann's helpful discussion of the psalm in *Israel's Praise*, pp.30–43.

150. Ibid., p.32.

151. J. Clinton McCann, *A Theological Introduction to the Book of Psalms* (Nashville: Abingdon Press, 1993) p.46.

152. Colin Morris, *Wrestling with an Angel* (London: William Collins, 1990) p.107.

153. Aidan Kavanaugh, *On Liturgical Theology* (Collegeville: The Liturgical Press, 1992) pp.153–4.

154. J. Clinton McCann, *A Theological Introduction to the Book of Psalms* (Nashville: Abingdon Press, 1993) p.46.

155. C.S. Lewis, 'The Grand Miracle' in ed. Walter Hopper, *Undeceptions: Essays on Theology and Ethics* (London: Geoffrey Bles, 1971) p.63.

Courses and events

Waverley Abbey College

Publishing and media

Conference facilities

Transforming lives

CWR's vision is to enable people to experience personal transformation through applying God's Word to their lives and relationships.

Our Bible-based training and resources help people around the world to:
• Grow in their walk with God
• Understand and apply Scripture to their lives
• Resource themselves and their church
• Develop pastoral care and counselling skills
• Train for leadership
• Strengthen relationships, marriage and family life and much more.

Our insightful writers provide daily Bible reading notes and other resources for all ages, and our experienced course designers and presenters have gained an international reputation for excellence and effectiveness.

CWR's Training and Conference Centre in Surrey, England, provides excellent facilities in an idyllic setting – ideal for both learning and spiritual refreshment.

CWR Applying God's Word
to everyday life and relationships

CWR, Waverley Abbey House,
Waverley Lane, Farnham,
Surrey GU9 8EP, UK

Telephone: +44 (0)1252 784700
Email: info@cwr.org.uk
Website: www.cwr.org.uk

Registered Charity No. 294387
Company Registration No. 1990308